Dim Sum

Dim Sum
Small bites made easy

HELEN & LISA TSE

Photography by
Gareth Morgans

Kyle Books

Dedication

This book is dedicated to God, Pastor Kim, Aunty Josephia and Brother Gery Christel Malanda Mbedi for your prayers, blessings, fellowship and guidance. This book is also dedicated to the Armitages and the Chumates for being simply amazing.

First published in Great Britain in 2015 by
Kyle Books
an imprint of Kyle Cathie Limited
192–198 Vauxhall Bridge Road
London SW1V 1DX
general.enquiries@kylebooks.com
www.kylebooks.com

10 9 8 7 6 5 4 3 2 1

ISBN: 978 0 85783 268 9

A CIP catalogue record for this title is available from the British Library

Text © Helen and Lisa Tse 2015
Photographs © Gareth Morgans 2015
Design © Kyle Books 2015

Editor: Vicky Orchard
Design: Dale Walker
Photography: Gareth Morgans
Food Styling: Joss Herd and Sunil Vijayakar
Props Styling: Polly Webb-Wilson
Production: Nic Jones and Gemma John

Colour reproduction by ALTA London
Printed and bound in China by Toppan Leefung Printing Ltd.

Contents

Foreword by Ken Hom

I was lucky enough to grow up eating dim sum, that wonderful and enormous variety of Chinese savoury and sweet snacks which are eaten between meals, for tea brunches and during banquets. Originally they were consumed only by members of the imperial household whose chefs concocted savoury delicacies such as minced pheasant dumplings and sweet ones made from steamed milk and sweet bean sauce. Over the centuries these and many less expensive versions have found their way into the diet of the ordinary Chinese. Even my aunt and mother made some very simple and tasty ones. Although most people have tasted dim sum in Chinese restaurants and think it is complicated and difficult to make little do they realise how easily it can be made at home. Helen and Lisa Tse's *Dim Sum* is, without a doubt, your best guide to these mouth-watering, delicious bites from one of the world's most popular styles of Chinese food. The clear and precise instructions are good enough to entice any cook into the kitchen to make what seems complicated simple. An amazing feat, indeed. The beautiful colour photos are enticing and the step-by-step photography gives you a feeling and confidence that Helen and Lisa are in the kitchen with you. I found the selection and choices of recipes and notes both helpful and insightful even to someone who has cooked and taught Chinese cuisine for so many years. It is quite obvious that many of the recipes and tips have come from their collective long experience of cooking and eating. I am certain your family and friends would be astonished and delighted with the results.

Without a doubt, Helen and Lisa have demystified and made accessible an intriguing and delectable part of one of the most ancient cuisines in the world. It is a book that belongs on every serious cook's kitchen shelf not only for cooking but for reference as well. I, for one, will find it an invaluable addition to my cookbook library and will treasure it with each delicious bite.

Introduction

'Teach me,' I begged the master dim sum chef.

'You are bold, for a girl,' he replied.

'Please teach me,' I said softly. 'Cooking has many layers and secret techniques. One wrong technique and you could bring my kitchen into disrepute.'

'I promise you, I'll work hard and be diligent,' I pleaded.

'One final thing,' the master dim sum chef replied, ' I am teaching you so you will help to keep this alive, so you can continue to share the legacy.' I bowed low. I was speechless, humbled and determined to be my best.

It is a truth universally acknowledged that a hungry person on a culinary adventure must be in want of dim sum. Well, that is the truth according to my grandma Lily Kwok, who taught me everything I know about the making,

cooking and eating of dim sum.

Dim sum translated literally means 'to touch your heart' and the art of making dim sum remains a secret to many people who love to cook Chinese food. At our Sweet Mandarin Cookery School, the dim sum masterclass remains oversubscribed for a year in advance. That is no surprise as there are over 2,000 dim sum recipes that range from easy to very hard. Helen and I decided to include a wide variety in this book – including some trickier recipes for those who like a challenge in the kitchen – together with step-by-step photographs that give an excellent picture of how to complete each stage. It is so much easier to compare your progress and technique to photographs than to words alone. I have written this book with Helen, and although I am the voice of the book, these recipes are ones that I have shared

with my sister and family. This book is the Sweet Mandarin Dim Sum Masterclass personified. Imagine Helen and me at your side in the kitchen guiding you along – pointing out useful techniques and giving you inspiring recipes to make you feel like a hero in the kitchen. This book will demystify the process and we hope your efforts will result in perfect dim sum every time.

Go to a Chinese restaurant on a Sunday afternoon and you will be greeted by a sea of Chinese families spanning three generations. Dim sum is the Chinese equivalent of French hors d'oeuvres or Spanish tapas. It's a colourful and loud dining experience starting with the rush for vacant seats and the hustle and bustle of the gesticulating waiters selling their dim sum specials from their trolleys. Bamboo containers filled with steamed dim sum are stacked high and quickly snapped up. Waiting staff ask what kind of tea you want to drink, offering a vast array of jasmine tea, oolong tea, pu'er tea and green tea, to help wash down the dim sum. The noise of the chatter of diners is deafening. It's a busy, frantic affair and there is an air of organised panic, which adds to the excitement and entertainment. Dim sum is an overwhelming introduction to the Chinese nation's love of food, gregariousness and cheerful chatter.

Dim sum mania spread to Hong Kong as the Guangzhou population immigrated to Hong Kong in the 1920s. Chinese restaurants grew exponentially in Hong Kong and soon dim sum was available from 6am through to late afternoon. Restaurants in Hong Kong and Guangzhou became filled mainly with the elderly population who often gathered to eat after the morning session of t'ai chi exercises, often enjoying the morning newspapers at the same time.

When Europe started trading with the Orient, the seaport of Guangzhou became the gateway to the West. The Chinese readily absorbed these cosmopolitan influences and, being great travellers themselves, emigrated to the United States of America and the United Kingdom. There they introduced Chinese cuisine to the Western world and in time dim sum became a firm favourite all over the world.

I love dim sum. There are over 200 dishes to choose from. One Cantonese saying goes that anything that walks, swims, crawls or flies is edible. Another says that the only four-legged things that Cantonese people won't eat are tables and chairs.

The range of cooking skills required to make dim sum is vast. In a restaurant, there is usually a dim sum master overseeing his section of the kitchen and there is a real art involved in making the dishes. Some dishes are steamed, others are fried, some are baked. The variety of tastes is mind-boggling – from sweet or sour to savoury and hot.

I learned the authentic recipes from Guangzhou and use them at Sweet Mandarin. Together with my sisters, Helen and Janet, we make every dim sum from fresh. Stuffing and shaping wontons is the real family enterprise. We make the stuffing from various fillings such as light prawn mince, chicken mince, minced pork or mixed pork and prawns and wrap the filling in a fine pastry of sorts. Each of us leaves our own individual stamp on the dim sum in the way we crimp the edges – I add a flamboyant tail on as many as I can, which can then be dipped in our sauces. My everyday rituals of properly selecting the produce, cooking and presenting a meal – all skills I have inherited from my family – have given me an insight into the meaning of my own cooking as a metaphor for life.

It is our honour to cook for you.

Lisa and Helen

Tweet us @SweetMandarins

Meat

肉類

Pork & Prawn Dumplings

燒賣

This dim sum is an open-topped steamed pork and prawn dumpling, called Siu Mai, which dates back to the Song Dynasty when it was traditionally served in teahouses along the Silk Road. Our mum has always believed that this was the first ever dim sum to be made for and eaten by the emperors of China, in particular Emperor Han who enjoyed Siu Mai as a mid-afternoon snack with Chinese tea. Although Siu Mai originate from Guangzhou, where rice is the staple diet, the dumpling skin is made from wheat flour to give a softer texture. The technique of folding and cooking the dumplings requires practice, but the test of a good Siu Mai is whether it can stand up when placed on a plate. The secret here is to use more filling than you would expect to fill the dumpling.

MAKES **12**
PREPARATION TIME **20 minutes**
COOKING TIME **10 minutes**

180g pork loin, cut into 1.5cm dice
250g raw, peeled king prawns,
**   deveined and finely chopped**
2 teaspoons salt
1 teaspoon white pepper
2 teaspoons caster sugar
1 tablespoon light soy sauce
1 tablespoon Shaoxing rice wine
2 tablespoons water
2 tablespoons potato starch
6 dried Chinese mushrooms,
**   finely diced**
3cm piece of fresh root ginger,
**   finely chopped**
1 spring onion, halved lengthways
**   and finely sliced**
1 tablespoon sesame oil, plus extra
**   for greasing**
12 wonton wrappers
12 garden peas (fresh or frozen),
**   to garnish**
Sweet Chilli Sauce (see page 156),
**   or soy sauce, to serve**

1 Put the diced pork in a large mixing bowl and set aside. Wash the king prawns and pat dry with kitchen paper. Place the flat blade of the knife on top of each king prawn and, using the base of the hand, crush the king prawn until it has the texture of a chunky paste. Once crushed, chop each king prawn into 4 pieces and repeat with the remaining prawns. Transfer to the bowl with the diced pork.

2 Add the salt, pepper, sugar, light soy sauce, Shaoxing wine, water and potato starch to the bowl with the pork. Mix with a metal spoon in a clockwise direction for 1 minute until thoroughly combined.

3 Add the diced mushrooms, ginger, spring onion and sesame oil. Mix in a clockwise direction for 2 minutes until the filling has a sticky consistency. Cover the bowl with clingfilm and transfer to the fridge to chill for 15 minutes.

4 Meanwhile, trim the corners off the wonton wrappers (with a knife or scissors) so that the pastry is round instead of square. To assemble the dumplings, cup the fingers on your left hand and place a wonton wrapper inside your cupped hand. Place 1 heaped tablespoon of the filling in the centre of the wrapper. Gather up the sides of the pastry around the filling and squeeze them together to form a little open-topped square parcel. Holding the Siu Mai between your thumb and index finger, carefully smooth the surface of the filling with a teaspoon or knife so that it is nice and level, and then place a pea in the centre. Arrange the filled dumpling on a lightly oiled plate and set aside while you assemble the rest.

5 Fill a wok with water so that it is just over one-quarter full. Set a round cake rack in the centre, cover with a lid and bring to the boil over a high heat. Place the plate of filled dumplings inside a bamboo steamer and steam in the wok for 10 minutes over a high heat. (Cook them in batches if necessary.) Open the lid slightly to allow some steam to escape for 2 minutes. Serve hot with Sweet Chilli Sauce or soy sauce.

 LISA'S TIP To ensure the dumplings stand upright don't be afraid to fill them generously. Arrange on a lightly oiled plate set slightly apart from one another to stop them sticking together.

Pan-fried Pork Dumplings
鍋貼

Our grandmother was a huge fan of this dish because the dumplings could be cooked in three different ways – boiled, steamed or fried. Her favourite cooking method was to deep-fry them as it gave a crunchy texture that contrasted nicely with the juicy, meaty centre. However, we prefer to pan-fry and steam them for a healthier taste. Wor Tiep are traditionally served during Chinese New Year because they resemble gold ingots. At home our grandmother used to have a long-held tradition where she hid a coin inside each dumpling – that is, until one got stuck in my throat and I had to be rushed to hospital! Thankfully the coin was coughed out, but that episode scared my grandmother so much that from then on she banned all coins from being hidden inside dumplings – even if it meant breaking the Chinese tradition.

MAKES **13**
PREPARATION TIME **25 minutes,**
plus 10 minutes resting time
COOKING TIME **7–8 minutes**

¼ Chinese cabbage, core removed,
  finely chopped
½ teaspoon salt
50g chives, finely chopped
300g minced pork
1 garlic clove, crushed
5cm piece of fresh root ginger, grated
1 tablespoon Shaoxing rice wine
½ tablespoon light soy sauce
1 teaspoon caster sugar
½ tablespoon oyster sauce
1 teaspoon sesame oil
2 tablespoons potato starch
1 tablespoon vegetable oil
50ml water
For the dumpling wrappers
110ml boiling water
½ teaspoon salt
200g strong white bread flour,
  plus extra for dusting
Chinese red vinegar and ginger
  strips, mixed together to form
  a dipping sauce, to serve

1 First make the dumpling wrappers. Measure the boiling water into a jug, add the salt and stir to dissolve. Sift the flour 2–3 times into a large mixing bowl, pour in the salted water and mix to a stiff dough with a wooden spoon. Turn out the dough onto a floured surface and knead for 10 minutes until smooth. Return the dough to the bowl, cover with a tea towel and set aside to rest at room temperature for 10 minutes.

2 Shape the dough into a long log and then divide into 13 pieces approx. 5cm wide. Roll into balls, flatten with the palm of your hand and roll out into 7–8cm circles using a rolling pin. Arrange the dumpling wrappers in a stack on a plate, dusting with flour between each wrapper, then cover with a clean tea towel and set aside.

3 To make the filling, place the chopped cabbage in a large mixing bowl and stir in the salt and chives. Leave the cabbage in the salt for 2–3 minutes, then squeeze the cabbage mixture in between your hands to extract as much water as possible and drain well. Return the cabbage to the mixing bowl and add the minced pork, garlic, ginger, Shaoxing wine, soy sauce, sugar, oyster sauce, sesame oil and potato starch. Mix well in a clockwise direction with a metal spoon until the filling is thoroughly combined and sticky in consistency.

4 To assemble the dumplings, wet your index finger with water and moisten the outer rim of a dumpling wrapper. Place 1 heaped tablespoon of filling in the centre of the wrapper and fold in half to form a half-moon shape. Seal the edge by pleating it from right to left. The best way to do this is to use your left thumb to push the wrapper to the right and use your right thumb and index finger to pinch the two layers of pastry together; this creates a nice wavy edge. Continue until the entire dumpling is sealed.

5 To cook the dumplings, heat the oil in a large, lidded frying pan over a medium heat. Add the dumplings and fry them for 1 minute on each side until they have a golden crust. Pour in the 50ml water, immediately cover the pan with a lid and cook until the water has evaporated, approx. 5–6 minutes. Reduce the heat to low then remove the lid and cook for a further minute. Serve the dumplings with Chinese red vinegar and ginger strips as a dipping sauce.

Shanghai-style Dumplings
with Pork, Ginger & Spring Onion
小笼包

These dumplings are known as Xiao Long Bao, which translates as 'little steaming baskets' and are one of Shanghai's most beloved snacks. As well as the meat filling there is also a small amount of soup that is sweet and packed with flavour, arguably the best bit.

MAKES **36**
PREPARATION TIME **1½ hours**,
plus **2 hours chilling time**
COOKING TIME **10 minutes**

For the stock
500g chicken wings
150g pork loin or spare ribs
5cm piece of fresh root ginger
4 whole garlic cloves, peeled
3 spring onions, roughly chopped
3 litres cold water
1 litre jasmine tea
1 tablespoon powdered gelatine
For the filling
3cm piece of fresh root ginger, grated
2–3 spring onions, finely diced
500g minced pork
1 teaspoon Shaoxing rice wine
1 teaspoon salt
1 teaspoon caster sugar
1 teaspoon sesame oil
2 tablespoons potato starch
For the dumpling wrappers
700g plain flour, plus extra
   for dusting
1 tablespoon vegetable oil
1 teaspoon salt
250ml boiling water
60ml ice-cold water
Chinese red vinegar and ginger
   strips, mixed together to form
   a dipping sauce, to serve

1 Put all the ingredients for the stock, except the powdered gelatine, in a large saucepan. Bring to the boil over a high heat, then reduce the heat to a simmer and cook for 30 minutes. Skim off any froth that rises to the surface using a slotted spoon.
2 Strain the broth through a sieve into a clean saucepan and skim the fat from the surface. Discard the chicken wings and other ingredients. Return the stock to a high heat and bubble away vigorously until reduced by half, approx. 10 minutes. Bring to the boil, add the powdered gelatine and mix well. Pour into a shallow container and cool, then transfer to the freezer for 2 hours. When frozen, cut into small cubes and transfer to the fridge; these cubes make it easier to place the stock inside the dumplings.
3 To make the filling, put all the ingredients in a large mixing bowl. Using a metal spoon, mix the ingredients together in a clockwise direction for 1 minute until thoroughly combined. Cover the bowl with clingfilm and transfer the filling to the fridge to firm up for 2 hours.
4 Meanwhile, make the wrappers. Put the flour, oil and salt in a mixing bowl, pour in the boiling water bit by bit then add the ice-cold water and mix well until thoroughly combined. The ice-cold water will reduce the temperature of the dough to stop it cooking. Turn out the dough onto a lightly floured surface and knead until smooth, approx. 10 minutes. The dough will feel quite moist and that's key to the pastry.
5 Split the dough into 3 equal logs approx. 36cm. Divide each log into 12 pieces so that you have 36 balls in total. Roll each piece into a ball and then flatten it with the palm of your hand to form a disc. Using a rolling pin, roll out each disc into a circle, approx. 8cm in diameter. Roll the pastry away from you, turn it clockwise by 45 degrees and then roll it away from you again – this should keep the wrappers nice and round.
6 To assemble the dumplings, place 1 heaped tablespoon of the chilled filling in the centre of each pastry circle, add one cube of frozen stock and gather up the edges to form an open money-bag shape. Carefully pleat the top edge by pinching the pastry together at intervals using your thumb and forefinger. Start at 3 o'clock and work the pleats anticlockwise until the opening in the middle becomes smaller. Close the top of each dumpling by twisting the pleated edge and pinching with your fingertips so that it is sealed tight.
7 To cook the dumplings, fill a wok with water so that it is just over one-quarter full. Line a bamboo steamer with baking parchment on top of the wok and arrange the dumplings inside, then steam for 10 minutes over a high heat. (Cook in batches if necessary.) Serve with Chinese red vinegar and ginger strips as a dipping sauce.

Shanghai-style Dumplings
with Pork, Aubergine & Miso
豬肉茄子醬香包

This is a new take on the traditional Shanghai Dumpling. I've added aubergine and miso to the pork filling, which makes this dim sum lighter and packed with umami flavours. The pleats keep the filling intact. If you don't have time to make the miso stock, replace it with instant miso soup, which is available from all good supermarkets.

MAKES **36**
PREPARATION TIME **1½ hours, plus
cooling and 1 hour chilling time**
COOKING TIME **10 minutes**

For the stock
800g chicken wings
150g pork loin or spare ribs
100g dried Japanese kelp
3 tablespoons white miso paste
1 tablespoon brown miso paste
10cm piece of fresh root ginger
4 whole garlic cloves, crushed
3 spring onions, roughly chopped
3 litres water
For the filling
2 aubergines
2cm piece of fresh root ginger, grated
2–3 spring onions, finely diced
500g minced pork
1 teaspoon Shaoxing rice wine
1 teaspoon salt
1 teaspoon caster sugar
1 teaspoon sesame oil
For the dumpling wrappers
700g plain flour, plus extra
    for dusting
1 tablespoon vegetable oil
1 teaspoon salt
250ml boiling water
60ml ice-cold water
Chinese red vinegar and ginger
    strips, mixed together to form a
    dipping sauce, to serve

1 Put all the ingredients for the stock in a large saucepan. Bring to the boil over a high heat, then reduce the heat to a simmer and cook for 20 minutes. Skim off any froth that rises to the surface using a slotted spoon.

2 Strain the stock through a sieve and discard the other ingredients. Transfer the stock into a clean saucepan and skim the fat from the surface. Return the stock to a high heat and bubble away vigorously until reduced by half, approx. 20 minutes. Pour into a shallow container and set aside to cool for 1 hour. Then transfer to the freezer for a further hour. When frozen, cut into small even-sized cubes and transfer to the fridge.

3 Meanwhile, char the aubergines over a gas flame until the skins blacken, approx. 2–3 minutes. (Alternatively, roast them in a hot oven at 180°C/gas 4 for 10 minutes.) Cut the charred aubergines in half and scrape out the flesh into a mixing bowl, discarding the skins. Add the ginger, spring onions, minced pork, Shaoxing wine, salt, sugar and sesame oil. Using a wooden spoon, mix the ingredients together in a clockwise direction for 1 minute until thoroughly combined. Then cover the bowl with clingfilm and transfer the filling to the fridge to firm up for 20 minutes.

4 Meanwhile, make the wrappers. Put the flour, oil and salt in a mixing bowl, pour in the boiling water bit by bit then add the ice-cold water and mix well until thoroughly combined. Turn out the dough onto a lightly floured surface and knead until smooth, approx. 10 minutes.

5 Split the dough into 3 equal logs approx. 36cm. Divide each log into 12 pieces so that you have 36 balls in total. Roll each piece into a ball and then flatten it with the palm of your hand to form a disc. Using a rolling pin, roll out each disc into a circle, approx. 8cm in diameter. Roll the pastry away from you, turn it clockwise by 45 degrees and then roll it away from you again.

6 To assemble the dumplings, place 1 heaped tablespoon of the chilled filling in the centre of each pastry circle, add one cube of frozen stock and gather up the edges to form an open money-bag shape. Carefully pleat the top edge by pinching the pastry together at intervals using your thumb and forefinger. Start at 3 o'clock and work the pleats anticlockwise until the opening in the middle becomes smaller. Close the top of each dumpling by twisting the pleated edge and pinching with your fingertips so that it is sealed tight.

7 Cook the dumplings in the same way as the Shanghai-style Dumplings with Pork, Ginger and Spring Onion (see opposite). Serve with Chinese red vinegar and ginger strips as a dipping sauce.

Pork Buns

叉燒包

There are two major kinds of Char Siu Bau: steamed and baked. Steamed Char Siu Bau has a white exterior, while its baked counterpart is browned and glazed. This recipe is for steamed char siu bau. Char Siu refers to the pork filling; the word 'bau' simply means 'bun'. Although visually similar to other types of steamed buns, the dough of steamed Char Siu Bau is unique because it uses both yeast and baking powder as leavening agents giving a slightly dense, but fine soft bread like texture. Encased in the centre of the bun is tender, sweet, slow-roasted pork tenderloin. This Char Siu is diced, and then mixed into a syrupy mixture of oyster sauce, honey, soy sauce, tomato purée, ginger, Shaoxing wine, sugar and potato starch.

The Char Siu Bau is extremely popular because it is delicious and exciting to open the bread and smell the aromatic sweet pork, then taste it. It originates from the Guangzhou region, which has popularised yum char or dim sum. The buns are usually enjoyed by many families on Sundays for yum char.

When we visited Hong Kong we tracked down our grandmother, Pop's, long-lost daughter, Ah Bing, who was the spitting image of our grandma. Since that meeting, and even after my grandmother's death, I've kept in touch with Ah Bing. For that trip Pop gave us a recipe enclosed inside an envelope for Char Siu Bau as she'd heard on the grapevine that it was Ah Bing's favourite dim sum. In turn, Ah Bing decided to share the recipe with us, since we were in the restaurant business, as she thought Pop would have wanted us to be the custodians of this precious recipe. I hope you enjoy it as much as our family does. There is something very special about it. As you break the 'bread' or the bun, you will be overwhelmed by the aromatic whiff of the caramelised pork and the sweetened sauce, which leaks into the white bun making every mouthful deliciously moreish.

MAKES **12**
PREPARATION TIME **1 hour, plus 4 hours marinating time**
COOKING TIME **10 minutes**

For the Char Siu
1kg pork neck fillet
1 teaspoon Chinese five spice powder
5 tablespoons runny honey
2 tablespoons tomato purée
3 tablespoons hoisin sauce
5 tablespoons light soy sauce
2 tablespoons vegetable oil

For the sauce
250ml boiling water
2 tablespoons runny honey
3 tablespoons oyster sauce
2 tablespoons light soy sauce
1 tablespoon tomato purée
2cm piece of fresh root ginger, grated
¼ teaspoon Chinese five spice powder
1 tablespoon caster sugar
1 tablespoon potato starch
1 tablespoon Shaoxing rice wine

For the dough
500g plain flour, plus extra for dusting
1 teaspoon salt
10g baking powder
2 teaspoons dried yeast
50g caster sugar
1 tablespoon sesame oil
260ml warm boiling water

LISA'S TIP **To make the dough more delicious leave it covered overnight so that it can expand even more.**

1 Place the pork in a large bowl, sprinkle over the five spice powder and rub it in well with your fingers.

2 To make the marinade, combine 3 tablespoons of the honey with the tomato purée, hoisin sauce, soy sauce and oil in a separate bowl. Pour three-quarters of the marinade over the pork and rub into the meat. Cover the bowl of pork with clingfilm and set aside in the fridge to marinate for at least 4 hours. Cover the remaining marinade with clingfilm and set aside in the fridge ready for basting the pork later.

3 Preheat the oven to 200°C/gas 6. Line a roasting tray with foil, pour in 150ml cold water and place a wire rack on top. Set the marinated pork on the wire rack and roast in the oven for 15 minutes. Remove the pork from the oven, baste all over with the reserved marinade and return to the oven for a further 15 minutes. Remove the pork from the oven and baste all over with the remaining 2 tablespoons of honey. Reduce the oven temperature to 180°C/gas 4 and return the pork to the oven for a further 15 minutes. Remove the roasted Char Siu from the oven and set aside to cool. Reduce the oven temperature to 110°C/gas ¼.

4 To make the sauce, combine all the ingredients in a medium saucepan and stir over a high heat until thick, approx. 10 minutes. Remove from the heat and set aside to cool. To finish the filling, cut half the cold Char Siu into 1cm dice and stir into the cold sauce. (Transfer the remaining Char Siu to the fridge and use for alternative dishes, such as Chinese Prok Puff Pastry Parcels, see page 30.)

5 To make the dough, sift the flour into a large bowl and stir in the salt, baking powder, yeast, sugar, sesame oil and warm water. Cover the bowl with clingfilm and set aside in the cool oven for 30 minutes until the yeast starts to ferment and the dough doubles in size.

6 Turn out the finished dough onto a lightly floured surface, cut into 2 equal pieces and roll into a log shape, approx. 30cm in length. Cut each log into 6 pieces, approx. 5cm in diameter, then roll into balls and flatten into discs with the palm of your hand. Using a rolling pin, roll out each disc into a circle, approx. 10cm in diameter.

7 To assemble the buns, cup the fingers of your left hand and place a circle of dough inside your cupped hand. Spoon 1 heaped tablespoon of the filling in the centre of the dough and use your right hand to gather up the edges of the dough into an open money-bag shape. Form the pleats by pinching the pastry together at intervals using the thumb and forefinger of your right hand. Start at 3 o'clock and work the pleats anticlockwise until the opening in the middle becomes smaller. Close the top of the bun by twisting the pleated edge together and pinching with your fingertips so that it is sealed tight. Reshape the buns into a rounded shape.

8 To cook the buns, fill a wok with water so that it is just over one-quarter full. Set a round cake rack inside, cover the wok with a lid and bring to the boil over a high heat. Line a bamboo steamer with baking parchment and arrange the buns inside, leaving a 2cm gap between each bun to allow for expansion – you might have to cook the buns in batches. Steam for 10 minutes. Remove from the heat and leave the lid of the steamer slightly ajar to allow some steam to escape for 2 minutes. Remove the buns from the steamer and serve hot.

Steamed Buns with Spicy Pork, Leek & Aubergine

辣肉茄香蒜包

Our grandmother taught me how to pair spicy pork with leek and aubergines, encasing them in a steamed bun to help keep the pork moist. This dish transports me back to my childhood days making these buns with my grandmother.

MAKES **12 buns**
PREPARATION TIME **1 hour, plus 1 hour rising time**
COOKING TIME **15–20 minutes**

2 aubergines
400g minced pork
2 medium leeks, cut into
   3cm matchsticks
1cm piece of fresh root ginger,
   finely chopped
1 teaspoon salt
pinch of white pepper
1 teaspoon caster sugar
1 teaspoon light soy sauce
1 tablespoon chilli bean paste
1 teaspoon black bean paste
1 teaspoon Shaoxing rice wine
1 teaspoon sesame oil
2 tablespoons potato starch
vegetable oil, for greasing
For the dough
500g plain flour, plus extra
   for dusting
2 teaspoons baking powder
2 teaspoons dried yeast
1 teaspoon salt
50g caster sugar
1 tablespoon sesame oil
260ml warm water

1 First make the dough. Sift the flour into a large mixing bowl. Add the baking powder, yeast, salt, sugar, sesame oil and warm water and mix together using a spatula until thoroughly combined. Turn out the dough onto a lightly floured work surface and knead with your hands until smooth, approx. 10 minutes. Place the dough back in the bowl, cover with clingfilm and set aside in a warm place to rise for 1 hour until doubled in size.

2 To make the filling, char the aubergines over a gas flame until the skins blacken, approx. 2 minutes. (Alternatively, roast them in a hot oven at 180°C/gas 4 for 10 minutes.) Cut the charred aubergines in half and scrape out the flesh into a mixing bowl, discarding the skins. Add the minced pork, leeks, ginger, salt, pepper, sugar, light soy sauce, chilli bean paste, black bean paste, Shaoxing wine, sesame oil and potato starch and mix with a metal spoon in a clockwise direction for 1 minute until thoroughly combined. Transfer to the fridge to chill for 30 minutes.

3 Turn out the dough onto a floured work surface and knead briefly until smooth. Roll into a 30cm log and split into 12 small pieces, approx. 5cm in diameter. Shape each piece into a ball and press each dough ball into a flat disc using the palm of your hand. Using a rolling pin, roll out the dough to form 12 circles, approx. 10cm in diameter. Place 1 heaped tablespoon of the filling in the centre of each circle and begin to pleat the top. Start at 3 o'clock and work the pleats anticlockwise until the opening in the middle becomes smaller. Close the top by twisting the pleats together and pinching with your fingertips. Transfer the finished buns to an oiled plate, spacing them apart from one another, ready for steaming.

4 Fill a wok with water so it is just over one-quarter full. Set a round cake rack in the centre, cover the wok with a lid and bring to the boil over a high heat. Line a bamboo steamer with baking parchment and place the buns inside, leaving 2cm gaps between the buns to allow them to expand. Steam in the wok for 10 minutes. (Cook them in batches if necessary.) Remove from the heat and leave the lid of the steamer slightly ajar to allow some steam to escape for 2 minutes. Remove the buns from the steamer and serve hot.

 LISA'S TIP **Always make sure the minced pork is fresh to help the mixture combine. If it is not fresh it often contains a lot of water, which will make the mixture too wet.**

Steamed Pork & Cabbage Buns

豬肉白菜包

I first came across these beauties when I got lost in a confusing maze of narrow, rabbit-warren-style side streets in Beijing. I had to choose whether to go left or right and literally followed my nose to the right. I smiled as I came across a stretch of street vendors who specialised in their own individual dim sum or noodle snacks. As I approached, one vendor lifted up his steamer lid – billowing steam escaped and I enjoyed the smell of the freshly cooked buns. I stopped there and then, smiling, because I couldn't wait to taste the buns. Steamed pork and cabbage work so well together and these buns make a wonderful alternative to a sandwich.

MAKES **10**

PREPARATION TIME **1 hour,**
plus 1 hour rising time

COOKING TIME **20 minutes**

5 dried Chinese mushrooms

5g dried shrimps

100g Chinese cabbage, shredded

3 spring onions, finely diced

2cm piece of fresh root ginger,
  finely chopped

500g pork loin, cut into 2cm dice

1 teaspoon salt

3 teaspoons light soy sauce

3 teaspoons oyster sauce

1 teaspoon Chinese five spice powder

1 tablespoon Shaoxing rice wine

pinch of white pepper

1 teaspoon caster sugar

1 teaspoon sesame oil

1 tablespoon potato starch

vegetable oil, for greasing

For the dough

350g plain flour, plus extra
  for dusting

15g baking powder

2 teaspoons dried yeast

1 teaspoon salt

40g caster sugar

1 tablespoon sesame oil

180ml warm water

1 First make the filling. Place the Chinese mushrooms and dried shrimps in a small bowl, cover with hot water and set aside to soak for 15 minutes. Remove the mushrooms and shrimps from the soaking liquor and squeeze out the water. Chop into very small pieces and set aside. Pour the soaking liquor into a jug and top up with boiling water to make 180ml stock, which you can use in the dough in place of the warm water if you wish. Set aside.

2 Place the cabbage, spring onions, ginger and pork in a mixing bowl and add the mushrooms and shrimps. Season with the salt, light soy sauce, oyster sauce, five spice powder, Shaoxing wine, pepper, sugar, sesame oil and potato starch. Mix with a wooden spoon in a clockwise direction for 3 minutes until thoroughly combined and sticky in consistency. Cover with clingfilm and transfer to the fridge to chill for 1 hour.

3 To make the dough, put the flour, baking powder, yeast, salt, sugar, sesame oil and water in a large bowl and mix together using a spatula to make a pliable dough. Turn out the dough onto a lightly floured work surface and knead with your hands for 10 minutes until smooth. Return the dough to the bowl, cover with clingfilm and set aside to rise in a warm place for 1 hour until doubled in size.

4 Remove the dough from the bowl on to a lightly floured work surface and knead lightly until smooth. Roll into 2 x 30cm logs and cut each into 5 even pieces. Shape each piece into a ball then press each dough ball into a flat circle, approx. 6cm in diameter, using the palm of your hand. Place 1½ heaped tablespoons of the filling in the centre of each circle and begin to pleat the top. Start at 3 o'clock and work the pleats anticlockwise until the opening in the middle becomes smaller. Close the top by twisting the pleats together and pinching with your fingertips. Transfer the finished buns to a bamboo steamer lined with baking parchment.

5 To cook the buns, fill a wok with water so that it is just over one-quarter full. Set a round cake rack inside, cover the wok with a lid and bring to the boil over a high heat. Place the bamboo steamer inside and steam for 20 minutes, leaving the lid of the steamer slightly ajar for the final minute of cooking. Serve hot.

Mini Chinese Sausage Buns

迷你腸仔包

I could not believe how many hot dog stands we walked past when we were in New York. The Chinese have an ingenious way of making their own version of traditional American dishes, so when I returned to the UK I was inspired to come up with my version of what is probably America's crown jewel in fast food – the hot dog. This recipe cooks the sausage inside the bun so that it doesn't fall out; I also find it's a great way of infusing more flavour into the bun. I cooked these as a treat for my niece's birthday party and she loved them.

MAKES **10**
PREPARATION TIME **30 minutes, plus
1 hour rising time**
COOKING TIME **15 minutes**

**400g plain flour
1 tablespoon dried yeast
2 tablespoons caster sugar
1 egg white
½ teaspoon white wine vinegar
200ml warm water
3 tablespoons lard, melted
10 long frankfurters**

1 Preheat the oven to 160°C/gas 3. Sift the flour into a bowl and stir in the yeast, sugar, egg white and vinegar. Add the warm water and melted lard slowly. Turn out the dough onto a floured work surface and knead with your hands until smooth, approx. 10 minutes. Return the dough to the bowl, cover with a damp tea towel and set aside to rise in a warm place for 1 hour until doubled in size.

2 Remove the dough from the bowl and roll out to form a 15cm square, approx. 8mm thick. Use a knife to cut the dough into 10 strips. To assemble the buns, place a frankfurter at one end of each strip and roll up to form a snail shape. Arrange the sausage rolls inside a bamboo steamer, lined with baking parchment, setting them apart from one another.

3 To cook the sausage rolls, fill a wok with water so that it is just over one-quarter full. Set a round cake rack in the centre, cover the wok with a lid and bring to the boil over a high heat. Place the bamboo steamer inside the wok and steam for 12–15 minutes. (Cook in batches if necessary.) Remove from the heat and leave the lid of the steamer slightly ajar to allow some steam to escape for 1 minute. Remove the buns from the steamer and serve hot.

 LISA'S TIP **Make sure you roll the pastry around the sausages without leaving any gaps. If any gaps show, push the ends of the pastry towards each other. These will then expand while steaming.**

Spring Rolls

春捲

Spring rolls are the nation's favourite dim sum, traditionally eaten during Chinese New Year celebrations because they resemble gold ingots – a symbol of wealth and power. One Chinese New Year, I remember Dad waving about ten of them in each hand – he'd definitely had too many beers – shouting, 'I'm going to get rich this year! Look how many gold bars I've got.' This was a time before there were such things as the Lottery. We were laughing so hard we had tears running down our faces. Dad never got rich that year but our New Year celebrations certainly started with a bang. These spring rolls are made with a pork filling, but you could substitute chicken or vegetables if you prefer.

MAKES **15**

PREPARATION TIME **55 minutes, plus 15 minutes marinating and 20 minutes cooling time**

COOKING TIME **10 minutes**

250g pork loin, cut into 4cm strips

10 dried Chinese mushrooms

2 tablespoons vegetable oil

250g beansprouts

50g rice vermicelli noodles, soaked and cut into 5cm lengths

1 teaspoon salt

1 teaspoon caster sugar

pinch of Chinese five spice powder

1 teaspoon light soy sauce

a drop of sesame oil

15 spring roll pastry wrappers

1 tablespoon plain flour and 1 tablespoon water, mixed together

vegetable oil, for deep-frying

Sweet and Sour Sauce (see page 156), to serve

For the marinade

½ teaspoon caster sugar

½ teaspoon salt

1 teaspoon light soy sauce

1 teaspoon Shaoxing rice wine

1 teaspoon sesame oil

1 tablespoon water

½ teaspoon Chinese five spice powder

1 Combine all the ingredients for the marinade in a large bowl. Add the sliced pork and mix well together. Cover the bowl with clingfilm and transfer to the fridge to marinate for 15 minutes. Place the Chinese mushrooms in a small bowl, cover with hot water and set aside to soak for 10 minutes; drain well, discarding the soaking liquor, and slice.

2 Meanwhile, heat a wok over a high heat and add 1 tablespoon of vegetable oil. Add the beansprouts, Chinese mushrooms, noodles, salt, sugar and five spice powder and stir-fry for 5 minutes. Tip out the cooked beansprouts onto a plate and set aside in a colander. Wash and dry the wok.

3 Return the wok to a medium heat with the remaining vegetable oil. Add the marinated pork and stir-fry for 8–10 minutes until cooked through. Return the beansprouts, mushrooms and noodles to the pan along with the soy sauce and sesame oil. Cook for 5 minutes, stirring. Strain through a colander to remove the excess moisture and set aside to cool for 20 minutes.

4 Separate the spring roll wrappers and start with the first sheet. Open up the sheet and turn it so that one corner is facing you, like a diamond. Place 1 heaped tablespoon of the filling towards the corner closest you. Bring the corner over the filling to enclose it and roll it forward, stopping at the middle. Brush (or spoon) a little flour-and-water paste on the remaining corners using a pastry brush (or spoon). Fold the left corner over the filling, followed by the right corner, and then roll up tightly to seal the spring roll. Repeat with the rest of the mixture to form 15 spring rolls in total.

5 To cook the spring rolls, fill a wok half full with vegetable oil and preheat over a high heat (to test the temperature, see page 149). Lower the spring rolls into the hot oil and cook for 6–7 minutes, turning constantly, until they are golden. Cook in batches and drain on kitchen paper. Serve with Sweet and Sour Sauce.

 LISA'S TIP **Make sure you wrap the spring rolls tightly into the shape of gold bars to prevent them from bursting when cooking in the hot oil.**

Chinese Pork Puff Pastry Parcels

叉燒酥

I made a plate of these for myself a few years ago and was really looking forward to tucking into them when service suddenly began and I forgot all about them. As midnight approached, I discovered my plate of Char Siu Sou waiting for me. Unfortunately they had gone cold, but I decided to eat them anyway – and much to my surprise I realised that while they are incredible hot, they are probably even more delicious cold. The filling almost melts into the pastry and the flavour of the pork intensifies once it cools.

MAKES **16**
PREPARATION TIME **45 minutes**
COOKING TIME **20 minutes**

1 tablespoon vegetable oil
1 garlic clove, crushed
1 small onion, finely diced
1 carrot, finely diced
2 tablespoons water
½ teaspoon salt
½ teaspoon sugar
1 teaspoon sesame oil
1 teaspoon oyster sauce
1 teaspoon Shaoxing rice wine
1 teaspoon potato starch mixed with
    2 teaspoons cold water to form
    a paste
350g cooked Char Siu (see pages
    20–22), cut into 3cm dice
plain flour, for dusting
1 beaten egg, to glaze
50g sesame seeds, to garnish
For the water dough
200g plain flour
1 tablespoon caster sugar
50g lard or shortening, diced
½ teaspoon vanilla extract
80–100ml water
For the oil dough
140g plain flour
85g hard lard or shortening, diced

1 To make the water dough, sift the flour into a bowl and add the sugar and mix well. Rub the lard into the mixture with your fingers until it resembles breadcrumbs. Add the vanilla extract and enough water mix them together to form a soft dough. Turn out onto a floured surface and knead until smooth, approx. 10 minutes. Return the dough to the bowl, cover with clingfilm and set aside to rest for 30 minutes.

2 To make the oil dough, sift the flour into a bowl and rub the lard into the mixture with your fingers, then mix together to form a soft dough. Turn it out onto a floured work surface and knead until smooth, approx. 10 minutes. Return the dough to the bowl, cover with clingfilm and transfer to the fridge.

3 To make the filling, heat a wok over a medium heat and add the vegetable oil. Add the garlic, onion and carrot and stir-fry for 2 minutes. Then add the water, salt, sugar, sesame oil, oyster sauce, Shaoxing wine and stir in the potato starch mixture. Add the Char Sui and mix well. Remove the pan from the heat and set aside for 15 minutes.

4 Preheat the oven to 200°C/gas 6 and line a baking tray with baking parchment. Dust your work surface with flour, remove the doughs from the bowls and cut each dough into 16 equal-sized round balls. Flatten the oil dough balls into discs approx. 5cm in diameter. Place one round ball of water dough in the centre of each oil dough disc. Close the dough to encase the water dough and form a small round dough ball. Flatten the stuffed round dough balls with a rolling pin and roll into approx. 7cm long shapes. Roll up the pastries so that they look like a Swiss roll, then turn the pastries 90 degrees and roll forward into small round dough balls again. Repeat this process three times. This will help give the pastries their crisp yet soft texture. After the third rolling, shape the final dough balls into round discs, approx. 7cm in diameter, using a rolling pin to make a thicker centre and a thinner rim.

5 To assemble the pastry parcels, place 1 heaped tablespoon of filling in the centre of each circle. Bring the pastry edges to the centre and close two edges first by using the thumb and index fingers. Then close the third and last edge. Once closed it should look like a triangle. Turn the completed pastry upside down so that you are looking at the smooth side.

6 Arrange the parcels on the prepared baking tray, brush the tops with beaten egg and sprinkle with sesame seeds. Bake for 20 minutes until golden. Serve hot or cold.

Steamed Pork in Bean Curd Sheets with Oyster Sauce

鮮竹卷

Bean curd is a unique ingredient that makes this dim sum really special. It has an al dente texture and absorbs the oyster sauce and steamed minced pork beautifully. Bean curd sheet can be bought at all good Asian supermarkets or online.

MAKES APPROX. **15**
PREPARATION TIME **20 minutes**
COOKING TIME **20 minutes**

10 dried Chinese mushrooms
2 tablespoons vegetable oil
1cm piece of fresh root ginger, grated
2 garlic cloves, crushed
400g minced pork
2 water chestnuts, finely diced
50g bamboo shoots, finely diced
1 medium onion, finely diced
3 spring onions, finely diced
100ml water
1 tablespoon oyster sauce
1 tablespoon light soy sauce
1 tablespoon rice vinegar
1 teaspoon salt
3 teaspoons caster sugar
½ teaspoon Chinese five spice powder
1 teaspoon sesame oil
3 tablespoons potato starch
200g packet of bean curd sheets
For the sauce
150ml water
2 tablespoons oyster sauce
2 teaspoons light soy sauce
1 teaspoon caster sugar
½ teaspoon salt
1 teaspoon Shaoxing rice wine
½ tablespoon potato starch mixed with 1 tablespoon water to form a paste
drop of sesame oil

1 First make the filling. Place the Chinese mushrooms in a small bowl, cover with hot water and set aside to soak for 10 minutes; drain well, discarding the soaking liquor, and cut into fine dice.

2 Heat a wok over a high heat and add 1 tablespoon of vegetable oil. Add the ginger and garlic and stir-fry for 1 minute until they release their fragrance. Add the minced pork and stir-fry for 3–4 minutes until the pork is cooked. Add the diced water chestnuts, bamboo shoots, onion, spring onions, mushrooms and water and continue to cook for 10 minutes, stirring. Season with oyster sauce, light soy sauce, rice vinegar, salt, sugar, five spice powder and sesame oil. Stir in the potato starch to thicken the sauce and cook for a further 5 minutes. Remove from the heat and set aside to cool.

3 Meanwhile, cut the bean curd sheets into 20cm squares. You will need approx. 15 thin sheets. To assemble the rolls, place 1 heaped tablespoon of the filling in the centre of each sheet and roll up to form a sausage shape, tucking in the ends.

4 Heat a wok over a low heat with the remaining 1 tablespoon of oil. Pan-fry the rolls, a few at a time, until they start to turn a light golden brown, approx. 5 minutes. Remove them from the pan and drain on kitchen paper while you fry the rest. Arrange the fried bean curd rolls inside a bamboo steamer lined with baking parchment.

5 Clean the wok and fill it one-quarter full with boiling water. Place a cake rack inside, cover the wok with a lid and bring the water to the boil over a high heat. Place the bamboo steamer inside the wok, reduce the heat to low and steam the bean curd rolls for 20 minutes.

6 Meanwhile, make the sauce by combining all the ingredients in a medium saucepan and stirring over a medium heat until reduced by one-third. To serve, arrange the steamed bean curd rolls on a serving plate and pour over the hot sauce.

 LISA'S TIP **You can also place the pan-fried bean curd rolls on a plate in a bamboo steamer, pour over the finished sauce and steam for 15 minutes.**

Sticky Rice Parcels

糯米雞

Whenever Mum serves Lor Mi Fan, she jokes that this glutinous rice is the cement that holds up the Great Wall of China. We used to find this hilarious, but when I visited China recently, and climbed the Great Wall, I was shocked to discover on the front page of the newspaper that chemical tests had indeed proved that parts of the wall's make-up were glutinous sticky rice! This dim sum is traditionally served as a symbol of love in China, typically to someone you secretly admire. In fact, I was actually presented with this dish on the Great Wall of China, by a tour guide who suddenly declared his undying love for me, much to the amusement of Helen! This type of rice is called glutinous rice (although it does not contain any gluten) and when cooked it will become sticky. This should be distinguished from over-boiled white rice, which goes wet and mushy. Glutinous rice has a distinctive nutty flavour and the great thing about it is that it absorbs other flavours like a sponge.

SERVE **2**
PREPARATION TIME **20 minutes, plus overnight soaking of the rice**
COOKING TIME **15 minutes**

200g glutinous rice
4 dried Chinese mushrooms
2 dried scallops
20 dried shrimps
1 spring onion
1 tablespoon vegetable oil
1 Chinese sausage (lap cheong), cut into 3cm dice
1 teaspoon oyster sauce
1 teaspoon light soy sauce
1 teaspoon Shaoxing rice wine
½ teaspoon salt
1 teaspoon caster sugar
1 teaspoon sesame oil
3 large lotus leaves, soaked in hot water for 10 minutes and halved

1 Rinse the rice really well in a sieve under cold running water. Tip into a bowl, cover with fresh water and set aside to soak for at least 12 hours, preferably overnight. Drain well.

2 Place the Chinese mushrooms in a small bowl, cover with hot water and set aside to soak for 10 minutes; drain well, discarding the soaking liquor, and cut into fine dice. Place the dried scallops in a separate bowl, cover with hot water and set aside to soak for 10 minutes; drain well, discarding the soaking liquor, and tear into small pieces. Place the dried shrimps in a separate bowl, cover with hot water and set aside to soak for 10 minutes; drain well.

3 Separate the green from the white stem of the spring onion and slice both very finely. Set aside on separate saucers. Heat a wok over a high heat and add the oil. Add the diced sausage, mushrooms, scallops, shrimps, oyster sauce, light soy sauce, Shaoxing wine, salt, sugar and sesame oil and stir-fry for 5 minutes. Remove from the heat and set aside.

4 Open up half a soaked lotus leaf and place 3 tablespoons of drained glutinous rice in the middle of the leaf. Add 3 teaspoons of the mushroom, sausage, scallop and shrimp mixture on top of the rice. Scatter over some diced spring onion. Roll the leaf forward to the centre. Fold the left- and the right-hand sides of the leaf to the centre. Continue rolling forward until all the leaf is encased in the parcel. It should resemble a large spring roll. Repeat with the remaining lotus leaves and mixture.

5 Arrange the parcels of glutinous rice inside a bamboo steamer lined with baking parchment. Fill a wok one-quarter full with boiling water. Place a cake rack inside, cover the wok with a lid and bring the water to the boil over a high heat. Place the bamboo steamer inside the wok and steam for 20 minutes over a medium heat. Serve hot.

Steamed Egg with Pork & Prawns

豬肉蝦仁蒸蛋

Our grandmother used to enjoy this dish for breakfast after t'ai chi classes while she was growing up in Hong Kong. I think the best part is drinking the juices because they're so sweet and delicious. The soft texture and saltiness of the pork and prawns make it perfect with steamed white rice.

SERVES **2**
PREPARATION TIME **15 minutes**
COOKING TIME **15 minutes**

4 large eggs
300ml chicken stock
1 teaspoon salt
1 teaspoon caster sugar
½ teaspoon sesame oil
4 teaspoons light soy sauce,
  plus extra for drizzling
200g minced pork
15 raw, peeled king prawns,
  deveined and finely diced
2 spring onions, finely diced

1 Using a fork, beat the eggs in a shallow metal container. Add the chicken stock, salt, sugar, sesame oil and soy sauce and stir in the minced pork and prawns until they are evenly distributed.

2 Fill a wok with water so that it is just over one-quarter full. Set a round cake rack in the centre, cover the wok with a lid and bring to the boil over a high heat. Reduce the heat to low and place the container of eggs inside the wok and steam for 10 minutes. The egg should still be slightly wobbly at this point. Then remove the lid, sprinkle over the spring onions, drizzle with some light soy sauce and steam for a further 5 minutes. Serve with steamed white rice.

 LISA'S TIP **If you haven't got chicken stock to hand use cooled boiled water to get the silky steamed egg.**

Steamed Pork Ribs with Black Beans

豉汁蒸去骨豬排

This is one of the most popular dim sum and one of our mum's favourites. She always tells us that the secret is to use pork rib meat on the bone as this contains all the umami flavours, which are released during steaming. The advantage of steaming the ribs, rather than roasting them, is that this cooking method makes the meat really tender – and it's healthier too – because the fat melts away from the meat.

MAKES **4 portions**
PREPARATION TIME **30 minutes,**
plus 20 minutes marinating time
COOKING TIME **15 minutes**

2 tablespoons vegetable oil
2 tablespoons fermented black beans
5 garlic cloves, finely chopped
2 spring onions, finely chopped
1 small red chilli, finely chopped
400g pork spare ribs, cut into 2.5cm
  lengths
For the marinade
4 tablespoons oyster sauce
3 tablespoons Shaoxing rice wine
3 tablespoons light soy sauce
1 tablespoon dark soy sauce
1 tablespoon caster sugar
1 teaspoon salt
8 tablespoons water
2 tablespoons potato starch
2 teaspoons vegetable oil

1 Heat a wok over a high heat and add the oil. Put in the black beans, garlic, spring onions and chilli and stir-fry for 5 minutes until they release their aroma.
Meanwhile, place the pork ribs in a large mixing bowl and add all the ingredients for the marinade. Stir well to coat the ribs in the marinade, and then scrape in the fried ingredients from the wok and mix well to combine. Cover the bowl with clingfilm and transfer to the fridge to marinate for 20 minutes.
2 Fill a wok with water so that it is just over one-quarter full. Set a round cake rack in the centre, cover the wok with a lid and bring to the boil over a high heat. Meanwhile, transfer the marinated pork, along with all the flavourings, to a heatproof container that will fit inside a bamboo steamer. To cook the ribs, place the bamboo steamer inside the wok and steam over a high heat for 10–15 minutes until cooked through. Serve with steamed rice.

 LISA'S TIP Fermented black beans are very salty, so use them sparingly; if you cannot find them they can be substituted with black bean sauce.

Steamed Beef Balls on Bitter Melon Rounds

涼瓜蒸牛丸

This was our Great-Aunt Yeep's favourite dish and is a lighter alternative to a Western meatball recipe, which typically consists of just meat and breadcrumbs. The addition of water chestnuts gives the meatballs a subtle crunch and fluffiness, while the bitter melon lends a pleasing sweetness to the finished dish.

MAKES **12**
PREPARATION TIME **20 minutes**
COOKING TIME **10 minutes**

vegetable oil, for greasing
3 bitter melons, sliced and cut into 3cm rounds
Barbecue Sauce (see page 156), to serve
For the meatballs
500g extra-lean minced beef
40g minced pork or bacon fat
2 strips of orange peel, soaked and minced, or orange zest
225g water chestnuts, finely diced
100g very finely chopped coriander
1 tablespoon soy sauce
1 tablespoon oyster sauce
1 tablespoon Shaoxing rice wine
½ teaspoon white pepper
1 teaspoon sesame oil
8 tablespoons water
2 tablespoons potato starch

1 Combine all the ingredients for the meatballs in a large mixing bowl and mix together in a clockwise direction for 3–4 minutes until thoroughly combined. This will break down the meat so that it becomes softer in texture.

2 To form the meatballs, scoop out a tablespoon of the mixture, then grease your hands with a little oil and shape into a perfectly round ball. Arrange the meatballs on the bitter melon rounds.

3 Fill a wok with water so that it is just over one-quarter full. Set a round cake rack in the centre, cover the wok with a lid and bring to the boil over a high heat.

4 Arrange the meatball-topped bitter melon slices on a heatproof plate that will fit inside a bamboo steamer. Place the plate inside the steamer and steam in the wok for 10 minutes over a high heat. Lift the lid so that it is slightly ajar for the final minute of cooking. Serve with Barbecue Sauce.

 LISA'S TIP **The filling mixture needs to be like a paste to give it that springy texture when steamed. Adding the orange peel gives the beef filling a delicious umami flavour.**

Meaty Spare Ribs in a Rich Noodle Broth

排骨湯麵

When we were growing up, Dad always used to come home tired and hungry after service at the takeaway. He used to flop into his favourite chair and then start greedily slurping on a bowl of this rich meaty broth with spare ribs and noodles, and he didn't surface for air until the last spoonful was finished. We always found it funny and used to giggle at him and take photos because the soup always splashed on his shirt. After a while he didn't care. It was all in the eating. Pure, unadulterated eating.

SERVES **4**
PREPARATION TIME **20 minutes**
COOKING TIME **1 hour**

200g thick fresh udon noodles
50g beansprouts
4 small sprigs of coriander, to garnish (optional)
For the stock
3 tablespoons vegetable oil
1 small onion, roughly chopped
400g spare ribs, cut into 5cm lengths
2 litres cold water
4 garlic cloves, peeled but kept whole
2 star anise
1 cinnamon stick
1 teaspoon white wine vinegar
1 tablespoon dark soy sauce
1 tablespoon caster sugar
½ teaspoon salt
1 long red chilli
4 tablespoons Shaoxing rice wine
4 x 2cm pieces of fresh root ginger
3 spring onions, finely sliced

1 First make the stock. Heat a large saucepan over a medium heat and add the vegetable oil. Put in the onion and ribs and stir-fry for 2 minutes until they start to colour. Add the water along with the rest of the ingredients for the stock and bring to the boil. Skim off any froth that rises to the surface using a slotted spoon. Reduce the heat and simmer for 30 minutes until the liquid has reduced by one-third.
2 Scoop out one ladle of stock, approx. 300ml, into a clean saucepan and bring to the boil over a medium heat. Put in the noodles and beansprouts and cook for 3 minutes.
3 To serve, divide the noodle and beansprout mixture between four serving bowls. Place two spare ribs in each bowl, pour over a ladleful of the hot stock and garnish with a sprig of coriander in each, if you wish.

Barbecued Beef Skewers

燒烤牛肉串

Barbecued Beef Skewers originated in the Xinjiang province of China and in recent years this dish has spread throughout the rest of the country, most notably to Beijing, Tianjin, and Jilin, where it is a popular street food. It is a product of the Chinese Islamic cuisine of the Uyghur people and other Chinese Muslims. The recipe comes from a street which is now called Muslim Snack Street, where men grill lamb marinated in cumin and red pepper over hot coals. The result: spicy, tangy and tender, is especially tasty during the cold winter months. In this recipe we have substituted lamb for beef.

MAKES **12 skewers**
PREPARATION TIME **20 minutes, plus**
1 hour marinating time
COOKING TIME **5 minutes, plus**
5 minutes resting

500g topside beef, cut into
   2.5cm cubes
50ml vegetable oil
1 teaspoon dried chilli flakes
1 teaspoon ground cumin
2 lemons, cut into wedges, to serve
For the marinade
80ml vegetable oil
1 teaspoon dried chilli flakes
1 teaspoon ground cumin
1 teaspoon grated nutmeg
1 teaspoon ground ginger
1 teaspoon ground coriander
3 garlic cloves, finely chopped
3 teaspoons sea salt
3 tablespoons light soy sauce

**You will need 12 wooden skewers,
soaked in water for 30 minutes**

1 Combine all the ingredients for the marinade in a large mixing bowl. Put in the chopped beef and mix thoroughly with your hands until evenly coated on all sides. Cover the bowl with clingfilm and transfer to the fridge to marinate for 1 hour.

2 Thread the beef onto the soaked wooden skewers, reserving the marinade in the bowl for later. Put a griddle pan over a low heat and add the oil. Cook the skewers for 1 minute on each side, turning continuously to prevent them burning and basting them with the reserved marinade as they cook.

3 Once the beef skewers have cooked, leave them to rest for 5 minutes to allow the juices to return to the meat. To serve, sprinkle with chilli flakes and ground cumin and accompany with the lemon wedges.

LISA'S TIP **Upgrade with sirloin steak and leave it slightly pink in the middle to make this dish even more juicy.**

Poultry

家禽

Boiled Jiozi Chicken Dumplings

雞肉水餃

We served these dumplings during the cook-off stages of the *F Word* Best Local Chinese Restaurant competition with Gordon Ramsay in 2009. We beat 10,000 other Chinese restaurants to be crowned the winner of Best Local Chinese Restaurant in the UK. It was a major achievement and wonderful to be acknowledged for what we love to do. In case you're thinking you can't make dough or dumplings, trust me – I've taught hundreds of students around the UK using this recipe and they have all passed the dumpling test. Have a go and tweet me your efforts (@SweetMandarins).

MAKES **8**

PREPARATION TIME **30 minutes, plus 30 minutes resting time**

COOKING TIME **25 minutes**

¼ Chinese cabbage, core removed, finely chopped

½ teaspoon salt

50g chives, finely chopped

200g minced chicken

1 garlic clove, crushed

10g fresh root ginger, grated

1 tablespoon Shaoxing rice wine

½ tablespoon light soy sauce

½ tablespoon oyster sauce

1 teaspoon sesame oil

1 tablespoon potato starch

1 teaspoon caster sugar

hot chilli oil, to serve

For the dumpling skins

110ml boiling water

1 teaspoon salt

200g strong white flour, plus extra for dusting

1 First make the dumpling skins. Pour the boiling water into a measuring jug, add the salt and stir to dissolve. Sift the flour 2–3 times into a mixing bowl. Pour the hot salted water over the flour and mix to a soft dough using a wooden spoon. Turn out the dough onto a floured board and knead until smooth, approx. 7–10 minutes. Shape the dough into two 20cm logs. Wrap separately in clingfilm and set aside to rest at room temperature for 30 minutes.

2 Cut each log into 4 pieces and shape into 8 balls. Flatten each one with the palm of your hand, and then roll into a 5cm circle using a rolling pin. Set aside in a stack on a plate, covered with a damp tea towel, while you make the filling.

3 To make the filling, place the cabbage in a large mixing bowl and stir in the salt and chives. Squeeze the cabbage mixture in between your hands to extract as much water as possible and drain well. Return the cabbage to the mixing bowl and stir in the rest of the ingredients for the filling. Mix well in a clockwise direction for 3 minutes until the ingredients are thoroughly combined and the mixture is sticky in consistency.

4 To assemble the dumplings, wet your index finger with water and moisten the outer rim of a dumpling skin. Place 1 semi-heaped tablespoon of the filling in the centre of each skin, and then fold in half to create a half-moon shape. Seal the edges by pleating from right to left. The best way to do this is to use your left thumb to push the wrapper to the right, and your right thumb and index finger to pinch the two layers of pastry together; this creates a nice wavy edge. Continue pleating until the entire dumpling is sealed. Repeat with the remaining wrappers and filling. Place the finished dumplings on a parchment-lined baking tray and transfer to the freezer for 10 minutes.

5 To cook the dumplings, fill a wok one-third full with water and bring to the boil over a high heat. Drop in the dumplings and cook for 20–25 minutes, stirring occasionally to stop them sticking together.

6 Remove the cooked dumplings from the wok using a slotted spoon and drain on kitchen paper to absorb the excess water. Serve with hot chilli oil.

Chicken Pastry Rolls

香蒜雞肉捲

This dim sum can be traced back to the Qing Dynasty (1644–1911). Weary travellers on the Silk Road would stop at teahouses for a pot of tea and a snack such as these rolls. Use chilled lard to make the pastry so that the dough can be easily kneaded; if the lard is warm it will make the dough too moist.

MAKES **12**
PREPARATION TIME **40 minutes**
COOKING TIME **20 minutes**

1 tablespoon vegetable oil
1 teaspoon crushed garlic
1 small onion, diced
1 carrot, diced
2 tablespoons water
½ teaspoon salt
½ teaspoon caster sugar
1 teaspoon sesame oil
1 teaspoon oyster sauce
1 teaspoon hoisin sauce
1 teaspoon Shaoxing rice wine
½ teaspoon potato starch mixed with
  2 teaspoons water to form a paste
150g cooked chicken breast fillets,
  diced into 2cm cubes
1 egg yolk, beaten, to glaze
50g sesame seeds
For the water dough
200g plain flour, plus extra
  for dusting
1 tablespoon caster sugar
50g lard or shortening, diced
100ml water
For the oil dough
140g plain flour
85g lard or shortening, diced

1 To make the water dough, sift the flour into a bowl and add the sugar and mix well. Rub the lard into the mixture with your fingers until it resembles breadcrumbs. Add the water and mix the together to form a soft dough, then turn out onto a floured surface and knead until smooth, approx. 10 minutes. Return the dough to the bowl, cover with clingfilm and set aside to rest for 30 minutes.

2 To make the oil dough, sift the flour into a bowl and rub the lard into the mixture with your fingers until it resembles breadcrumbs. Turn it out onto a floured surface and knead until smooth, approx. 10 minutes. Return the dough to the bowl, cover with clingfilm and transfer to the fridge.

3 While the dough is resting, prepare the chicken filling. Heat a wok with the vegetable oil over a high heat. Stir-fry the garlic, onion and carrot for 2 minutes. Add the water, salt, sugar, sesame oil, oyster sauce, hoisin sauce, Shaoxing wine and potato starch mixture. Mix well. Add the diced chicken and mix well. Remove from the heat and leave to cool for 15 minutes.

4 Preheat the oven to 200°C/gas 6 and line a baking tray with baking parchment.

5 Dust a work surface with flour, remove the doughs from the bowls and cut each dough into 12 equal-sized round balls. Flatten the oil dough balls into discs approx. 5cm in diameter. Place one round ball of water dough in the centre of each oil dough disc. Close the dough to encase the water dough and form a small round dough ball. Flatten the stuffed round dough balls with a rolling pin and roll into approx. 7cm long shapes. Roll up the pastries so that they look like a Swiss roll, then turn the pastries 90 degrees and roll forward into small round dough balls again. Repeat this process three times. This will help give the pastries their crisp yet soft texture. After the third rolling, shape the final dough balls into round discs, approx. 7cm in diameter, using a rolling pin to make a thicker centre and a thinner rim.

6 To assemble the pastry parcels, place 1 semi-heaped tablespoon of chicken filling in the centre of each circle. You want to aim for a round shaped pastry. Close the edges by pleating the edges starting from 12 o'clock and working around the pastry until it is completely closed. Turn the completed round pastry upside down so that you are left with the smooth side. Score the surface with three diagonal lines.

7 Arrange the finished rolls on a baking tray, brush the tops with beaten egg, scatter with sesame seeds and bake in the oven for 20 minutes until puffed up and golden. Serve hot, straight from the oven.

Chicken, Mushroom & Wild Rice Parcels

荷葉蘑菇糯米雞

The wild card in this dim sum is the wild rice. When I was told about 'wild' rice as a child, it conjured up a jungle of sheaths of rice of differing colours and heights looking fierce and exotic. I had been brought up on white rice, which nutritionally speaking is just starch and nothing much else, but wild rice carries an abundance of B vitamins, which help keep the nervous system in check and convert the foods we digest into fuel for the body. The sweetness from the chicken and the umami flavours from the mushrooms absorb beautifully into the wild rice.

SERVES **2–3**
PREPARATION TIME **20 minutes,**
plus overnight soaking and 15 minutes
marinating time
COOKING TIME **15 minutes**

200g wild rice
200g glutinous rice
500g skinless chicken breast fillets,
  cut into 3cm strips
2 teaspoons salt
2 teaspoons caster sugar
9 tablespoons water
1 tablespoon potato starch
10 dried Chinese mushrooms
30g dried shrimps
1 tablespoon vegetable oil
1 Chinese sausage (*lap cheong*),
  cut into 2cm dice
1 tablespoon oyster sauce
1 tablespoon Shaoxing rice wine
1 teaspoon sesame oil
1 spring onion (white part only),
  finely sliced
6 lotus leaves

1 Rinse the both types of rice really well in a sieve under cold running water. Tip into a bowl, cover with fresh water and set aside to soak for at least 12 hours, preferably overnight. Drain well.

2 Place the chicken in a bowl and stir in 1 teaspoon of salt, 1 teaspoons sugar, 3 tablespoons of water and the potato starch. Cover the bowl with clingfilm and set aside in the fridge to marinate for 15 minutes.

3 Meanwhile, place the Chinese mushrooms and dried shrimps in a bowl, cover with hot water and set aside to soak for 15 minutes. Drain well and cut into small pieces, discarding the soaking liquor.

4 Fill a medium saucepan with water and bring to the boil over a high heat. Add the marinated chicken strips and simmer gently for 10 minutes until cooked through. Drain in a colander and refresh under cold running water.

5 Heat a wok over a high heat and add the oil. Put in the diced sausage, mushrooms, shrimps and cooked chicken and stir-fry together for 5–10 minutes. Add the drained wild rice and continue to stir-fry for 10 minutes. Add the water, oyster sauce, Shaoxing wine, salt, sugar and sesame oil, reduce the heat and simmer for approx. 30 minutes until the rice has softened. If the rice is still hard after this time, add 10 tablespoons of water and continue to cook for a further 5–10 minutes. Finally add the spring onion and stir-fry for 2 minutes.

6 To assemble the parcels, split the lotus leaf into 5–6 equal parts. Scoop out one-quarter of the wild rice mixture and place in the centre of each leaf. Fold in the left-hand edge over the filling and then the right hand edge and roll forward to close the leaf. The finished parcels should be approx. 5cm x 3cm.

7 Fill a wok with water so that it is just over one-quarter full. Set a round cake rack in the centre, cover the wok with a lid and bring to the boil over a high heat. Place the lotus leaf parcels inside a bamboo steamer lined with baking parchment and steam for 15 minutes. Serve hot.

 LISA'S TIP When cooking the rice in the wok ensure the heat is low and add the water bit by bit, which will soften the rice. When steaming, the rice will continue to cook and expand but not become mushy.

Chicken's Feet

I know the idea of eating chicken's feet can sound unappealing, but trust me – they are good. They are no more adventurous than oxtail or pig's trotters, which have become very popular in Michelin-star restaurants. These little brown feet are deep-fried, then braised in a sweet, ginger sauce. This recipe is a wonderful source of calcium and collagen – perfect for maintaining firmness and moisture in your skin.

SERVES **4**
PREPARATION TIME **40 minutes**
COOKING TIME **45 minutes**

24 chicken's feet
500ml vegetable oil for deep-frying,
   plus 2 tablespoons
2 teaspoons distilled white vinegar
1 garlic clove, finely chopped
4 x 2cm pieces of fresh root ginger,
   cut into thin strips
1 teaspoon chilli bean sauce
2 teaspoons black bean garlic sauce
15 black beans
1 small red chilli, cut into thin strips
250ml water
1 teaspoon Shaoxing rice wine
1½ teaspoons runny honey
½ teaspoon salt
1 teaspoon sesame oil
1 tablespoon oyster sauce
1 teaspoon light soy sauce
1 teaspoon dark soy sauce
1 tablespoon potato starch

1 Clean the chicken's feet with water and chop off the nails with a sharp knife. Put the cleaned feet in a large saucepan and fill to the top with water. Add 1 tablespoon of vegetable oil and the vinegar. Bring to the boil over a high heat and cook for 15 minutes, then drain through a colander and refresh under cold running water. Blot dry on kitchen paper to remove excess moisture (otherwise they will splatter when you deep-fry them).

2 Preheat the vegetable oil to 180°C in a wok over a high heat (to test the temperature, see page 149). Deep-fry the chicken's feet in the hot oil for 8–10 minutes until golden brown. Remove them with a slotted spoon and set aside to soak in a bowl of cold water for 10 minutes.

3 Heat a clean wok over a high heat and add the remaining 1 tablespoon of oil. Put in the garlic and ginger and stir-fry for 1 minute. Then add the chilli bean and black bean sauces, the black beans and chilli and cook for a further 5 minutes. Add the cooked chicken's feet and remaining ingredients and cover and cook for 10 minutes, stirring well. Remove the lid, give the mixture a quick stir and simmer gently until the sauce has reduced by a quarter, approx. 5–10 minutes. (If the sauce reduces too much, you could thin it down with a little water.)

4 Meanwhile, fill a clean wok with water so that it is just over one-quarter full. Set a round cake rack in the centre, cover the wok with a lid and bring to the boil over a high heat. To finish the dish, place 3–4 of the fried chicken's feet in a small heatproof dish that will fit inside your steamer. Pour over 2 tablespoons of the sauce and transfer the bowl to a bamboo steamer. Steam in the wok for 10 minutes over a high heat. Serve with steamed rice.

 LISA'S TIP This dim sum focuses on the tenderness of the chicken skin. It's important to make sure the chicken's feet are boiled over a high heat and constantly covered with water.

Chicken Noodle Soup

雞肉湯麵

Chicken Noodle Soup is the folklore remedy for a cold because the soup has an anti-inflammatory effect, which can temporarily ease the symptoms of a cold. This is home cooking at its simplest and best. Typically the old chickens (that no longer lay eggs) are used for this soup as they are fattier and therefore enhance the flavour of this soup. Noodles are added to make the soup a more substantial and complete meal.

SERVES **4**
PREPARATION TIME **1 hour 20 minutes**
COOKING TIME **15 minutes**

24 chicken wings
300ml water
1 small onion, roughly chopped
2cm piece of fresh root ginger
1 spring onion, finely sliced
1½ teaspoons salt
8 chicken thighs
1 small head of broccoli, cut into
  small florets
2 x 200g packs of Hokkien noodles
1 teaspoon oyster sauce
1 teaspoon caster sugar
1 teaspoon Shaoxing rice wine
2 teaspoons light soy sauce
1 teaspoon sesame oil
2 bunches of pak choi, leaves
  separated
chilli oil, to serve

1 Preheat the oven to 200°C/gas 6. Put the chicken wings, water, onion, ginger, spring onion and 1 teaspoon of the salt in a large saucepan and bring to the boil over a high heat. Reduce the heat and simmer for 1 hour to make a stock. Skim off the scum from the surface of the stock using a slotted spoon.

2 Meanwhile, put the chicken thighs on a baking tray and scatter over a pinch of salt. Bake for 15–20 minutes until golden. Remove from the oven and set aside.

3 Strain the chicken stock into a wok, discarding the bones and flavourings. Bring to the boil over a high heat and add the broccoli florets. Cook for 5 minutes. Add the Hokkien noodles and cook for a further 10 minutes. Remove the noodles and broccoli from the wok and distribute evenly among 4 bowls. Then add the oyster sauce, sugar, the remaining ½ teaspoon of salt, Shaoxing wine, light soy sauce and sesame oil to the wok. Add the pak choi and blanch for 4 minutes. Remove the pak choi and divide it evenly among the 4 bowls. Place 2 cooked chicken thighs on top of the noodles in each bowl and pour over the stock so that it just covers the noodles. Serve with chilli oil.

 LISA'S TIP You can rinse the noodles in cold water to stop them overcooking. Once you add the hot chicken stock to the bowls their springy texture will return.

Jasmine Tea & Honey Chicken Skewers

茶香雞

Jasmine tea is scented with the perfume of jasmine blossoms to make a fragrant tea. Typically made with green tea as the base, it is probably the most famous scented tea in China. The jasmine plant is believed to have been introduced into Chinese teahouses from Persia via India along the Silk Road during the Han Dynasty (206 BC to 220 AD). The aromatic flavour of jasmine tea goes particularly well with chicken, giving these skewers a subtle, sweet taste and a distinctive, smoky flavour.

MAKES **16 skewers**
PREPARATION TIME **10 minutes, plus
45 minutes marinating time**
COOKING TIME **5 minutes**

200g skinless chicken breast fillets
sesame seeds, to garnish
4 tablespoons vegetable oil
For the honey and jasmine tea glaze
10g loose Jasmine tea leaves
50ml boiling water
4 tablespoons runny honey
2 teaspoons yellow mustard
½ teaspoon salt
1 teaspoon sugar
1cm piece of fresh root ginger, grated
1 tablespoon sesame oil

**You will need 16 wooden skewers,
soaked in water for 30 minutes**

1 First make the glaze. Place the tea leaves in a jug, pour over the boiling water and set aside to steep for 3 minutes. Strain into a small bowl, discarding the leaves, and stir in the honey, mustard, salt, sugar, ginger and sesame oil. Pour 5 tablespoons of glaze into a separate bowl and set aside.

2 Slice the chicken breasts in half, and then lengthways into 3cm 'ribbons'. Halve each ribbon. Place the chicken in the honey and jasmine tea glaze. Cover the bowl with clingfilm and set aside in the fridge to marinate for 45 minutes.

3 Meanwhile, weave the ribbons of marinated chicken onto 16 wooden skewers.

4 In a dry pan over a medium heat carefully toast the sesame seeds for 1 minute until they start to brown. Set aside.

5 Heat a frying pan with 2 tablespoons of oil over a medium heat and add the skewers. Cook the skewers on each side for 30 seconds. They will cook very quickly so use tongs to turn them frequently. Preheat a griddle pan over a high heat and add the remaining 2 tablespoons of oil. Transfer the skewers to the griddle pan and slightly sear them on each side for 20 seconds.

6 To serve, sprinkle the chicken skewers with the toasted sesame seeds and accompany with a small amount of the reserved glaze.

 LISA'S TIP Using a griddle pan can easily burn this dish so an alternative is to grill the skewers for 5–8 minutes in the oven.

Chicken Wings Braised in Cola

可樂雞翅

My grandmother used to prepare this dish when we were young and make us guess what the secret ingredient was – we had no clue it was cola. These wings are cooked using the braising technique, which softens the flesh causing the meat to fall off the bones and caramelise in the cola, changing the flavour of this soft drink into a nice, sweet gravy. This dish is as sweet as that moment when I first tried it.

SERVES **2**
PREPARATION TIME **10 minutes, plus
30 minutes marinating time**
COOKING TIME **15 minutes**

**800g chicken wings
4 tablespoons light soy sauce
2 garlic cloves, crushed
2cm piece of fresh root ginger,
  grated
200ml boiling water
2 tablespoons vegetable oil
330ml cola
½ teaspoon sesame oil
1 spring onion, finely diced**

1 Mix the chicken wings with the light soy sauce, garlic, ginger and water in a bowl. Cover with clingfilm, then cool and transfer to the fridge to marinate for 30 minutes.
2 Heat a wok over a high heat, add the vegetable oil and pan-fry the marinated chicken wings for 7–8 minutes on each side until golden. Pour in the cola and 100ml of the marinade, reduce the heat and simmer gently until the liquid has reduced by one-third, approx. 10 minutes. Add the sesame oil. Garnish with the diced spring onion and serve immediately.

 LISA'S TIP Marinating the chicken first means that the chicken wings are moist and not overly dry when re-cooking them in the cola mixture.

Chinese Porridge with Chicken

中式雞粥

Whenever I eat congee – a thick porridge made with rice that has disintegrated after hours of slow cooking in water – it reminds me of my grandmother. She used to make it for me for breakfast and when I was ill, saying that it would build up my constitution. I remember how she used to fill my head with stories about how congee was served during times of famine in China and how her father had to stretch the rice supply to feed the entire family. 'And, yet, look at me now!', she would say, making a Popeye gesture and rubbing her fat belly. We both laughed as we tucked into our bowls of 'jook', as she called it, the Cantonese slang for congee. Later on, when I was older, it was over a bowl of congee that I broke the news to her that we were giving up our careers to set up a family restaurant. Mum had hit the roof when I told her and I was waiting for a similar response from Pop. But, slurping on her congee, she just smiled at me, saying: 'You have my blessing. Do it, and do it well ... I'll deal with your mum.'

PREPARATION TIME **20 minutes, plus 1 hour soaking/marinating time**
COOKING TIME **1½ hours**

400g long grain rice
1.2kg chicken, skin removed
**2 teaspoons salt, plus extra
   for seasoning**
4–5 dried scallops
8 litres water
3 spring onions, finely diced
prawn crackers, to serve

1 Wash the rice in a sieve under cold running water and drain well. Repeat this process three times or until the water runs clear rather than cloudy. Set aside.
2 Rub the chicken with salt and set aside for 10 minutes.
3 Place the dried scallops in a bowl, cover with hot water and set aside to soak for 10 minutes; drain well, discarding the soaking liquor, and tear into small pieces.
4 Put the rice and water in a large saucepan over a medium heat, bring to the boil and cook for 20 minutes.
5 Meanwhile, wash the chicken then add it to the saucepan and stir together with the rice. Bring to the boil then reduce the heat to medium, stirring continuously. Cover with a lid left slightly ajar to let the steam escape and cook for a further 40 minutes, stirring every 5 minutes.
6 Remove the chicken from the pan and shred into fine slices. Return to the pan with the spring onions and add the scallops. Season with salt to taste. Cook over a low heat for a further 15 minutes. Serve with prawn crackers to dip into the congee.

 LISA'S TIP The trick when making congee is to stir continuously with a flat-based spatula to prevent the rice sticking to the bottom of the pan.

Chicken & Mushrooms with Fragrant Rice

冬菇蒸雞飯

We used to be so envious of our teenage friends when we were growing up. While they were having house parties and going out, we were expected to return from school to our chippy like clockwork ready to cook for and serve our customers. However, all our worries and frustrations seemed to evaporate when we grabbed a 'chicken and mushroom pie' Chinese-style. I regard myself as British, but in cuisine terms I am totally immersed in Chinese cooking. So imagine my joy when I learnt how to make this classic British dish using the Chinese staple ingredient of rice. This recipe is so easy to make and packed with flavour – and it's a healthier option than pie too.

SERVES **2**

PREPARATION TIME **40 minutes, plus 30 minutes marinating time**

COOKING TIME **1 hour 20 minutes**

6 skinless boneless chicken thighs,
  cut into 2cm slices
4 x 3cm slices of fresh root ginger
2 tablespoons light soy sauce
1 teaspoon dark soy sauce
1 teaspoon caster sugar
1 tablespoon potato starch
1 tablespoon Shaoxing rice wine
10 dried Chinese mushrooms
300g Thai fragrant rice
drop of sesame oil
1 spring onion, finely sliced

1 Place the sliced chicken in a bowl, add the ginger, soy sauces, sugar, potato starch and Shaoxing wine and mix well together. Cover the bowl with clingfilm and transfer the chicken to the fridge to marinate for 30 minutes.

2 Meanwhile, place the Chinese mushrooms in a bowl, cover with warm water and set aside to soak until soft, approx. 15 minutes. Drain well, discarding the soaking liquor, and cut them in half if they're big.

3 Wash the rice in a sieve under cold running water and drain well. Repeat this process twice or until the water runs clear rather than cloudy. Tip the rice into a bowl that will fit inside a steamer and cover with water. To work out the correct amount of water, place your hand in the pan so that the base of the third finger touches the top of the rice. Top up the water so that it is level with the second knuckle on the third finger.

4 Fill a wok with water so that it is just over one-quarter full. Set a round cake rack in the centre, cover with a lid and bring to the boil over a high heat. Place the bowl inside a bamboo steamer and steam in the wok for 10 minutes over a high heat until half the water has been absorbed into the rice.

5 Drain the marinated chicken, discarding the marinade and add to the bowl in the steamer. Add the mushrooms and steam for a further 15 minutes. To serve, add a drop of sesame oil and sprinkle with spring onion on top.

 LISA'S TIP You can also use the rice to stuff large Chinese cabbage leaves. Blanch the leaves in hot water for 2 minutes then drain. Stuff with the rice mixture and serve as a parcel – delicious!

Duck Filo Baskets
鴨肉特餐

This dim sum will really impress your guests, and the advantage is it can be assembled in advance to give you a chance to enjoy the party rather than slaving over the stove. The crunchy texture of the filo basket is a throwback to the idea of crispy duck, but in a bite-sized, dim sum format.

MAKES **24 canapés**
PREPARATION TIME **20 minutes**
COOKING TIME **10 minutes**

4 spring roll pastry wrappers
200g roast duck meat, shredded
¼ cucumber, peeled and cut into
**   1cm dice**
50g edamame beans
2 tablespoons hoisin sauce mixed
**   with 1 tablespoon water**
1 tablespoon lime juice
toasted sesame seeds (see Lisa's Tip),
**   to garnish**

You will need 2 x 12-bun muffin tins

1 Preheat the oven to 190°C/gas 5. First prepare the pastry baskets. Cut the pastry into 24 rounds using a 4cm pastry cutter and use to line the holes of 2 x 12-bun muffin tins. Bake for 5 minutes until golden and crisp. Remove from the oven and set aside to cool in the tins.

2 To make the filling, combine the shredded duck, diced cucumber, edamame beans, hoisin sauce mixture and lime juice in a bowl and mix well together. Divide the mixture among the cooked pastry shells and garnish with toasted sesame seeds. Delicious paired with a glass of Merlot.

 LISA'S TIP To toast the sesame seeds cook them in a dry pan over a medium heat for no more than 2 minutes. Any longer and they can easily burn.

Fish & Seafood

魚和海鮮

Honey Sesame Salmon & Tomato Kebabs

蜂蜜烤三文魚串

These kebabs are a great dim sum for parties as they are easy to eat and look very appealing. The combination of the salty salmon with a hint of honey and the crunch and aroma of sesame seeds really make this dish special. Our grandmother used to make these for our birthday. She said the secret ingredient was the sesame seed: 'Just because they are small, don't under estimate these', she'd lecture, waving her fat finger at us. 'These sesame seeds can save lives – they are rich in minerals ... like zinc, iron, calcium and potassium – so be generous. Your mum needs an extra dose.' Mum has arthritis and I now make this dim sum for her when she takes a turn for the worst because these minerals have anti-inflammatory action, helping to reduce her painful, swollen joints.

MAKES **12 kebabs**
PREPARATION TIME **15 minutes, plus**
30 minutes marinating time
COOKING TIME **10 minutes**

550g skinless salmon fillet
2 teaspoons sea salt
500g cherry tomatoes
6 courgettes, cut into 2cm rounds
rocket leaves and lime wedges,
  to serve
For the marinade
5 tablespoons clear honey
2 tablespoons Shaoxing rice wine
1 teaspoon light soy sauce
juice of 1 lime
1 teaspoon sesame oil
½ teaspoon dried chilli flakes

You will need 12 wooden skewers,
soaked in cold water for 30 minutes

1 Cut the salmon into 3cm cubes and season all over with the salt. Combine the ingredients for the marinade in a small bowl.

2 Thread the cubes of salmon onto the wooden skewers, alternating them with the tomatoes and courgettes. Using a pastry brush, baste the kebabs with some of the marinade and arrange on a plate. Cover with clingfilm and transfer to the fridge to marinate for 30 minutes.

3 Preheat the oven to 180°C/gas 4 and place the skewers on a baking tray. Bake for 10 minutes, turning the kebabs so that they are cooked evenly. Serve on a bed of rocket accompanied by wedges of lime.

 LISA'S TIP You can also griddle the kebabs for 3–4 minutes but they cook very quickly so constantly keep an eye on them to prevent burning.

Chinese-style Fish Balls in Homemade Broth

魚丸湯

Support your local fishmonger or farmer's market and buy fresh fish for these Chinese-style fish balls. Once the fish is taken home, washed and cooked there is no trace of that fishy smell anymore – just delicious dim sum in a hearty broth.

SERVES **4 (Makes 24 balls)**
PREPARATION TIME **20 minutes, plus**
30 minutes resting time
COOKING TIME **15 minutes**

600g skinless firm, white fish fillet, such as cod, haddock, hake, sea bass or halibut
1 tablespoon egg white
1 teaspoon salt
1 tablespoon tapioca starch
2 tablespoons potato starch
300ml chicken stock
2 heads of pak choi, split into individual leaves
a drop of sesame oil

1 Combine the fish, egg white, salt, tapioca and potato starch in a food processor and blitz to a smooth paste, thinning it with 1–2 tablespoons of water if necessary.
2 The next step is to make the fish balls' elastic texture. Wet your hands under a cold tap, scoop out the fish paste into your hands, and then throw it back into the bowl. Repeat this process at least 10 times until the fish paste firms up. Cover the bowl with clingfilm and transfer the mixture to the fridge to rest for 30 minutes.
3 To shape the fish balls, remove a heaped teaspoon of the fish mixture at a time and roll it into a small grape-sized balls in the palms of your hands. Arrange the fish balls on a plate.
4 To cook the balls, pour 300ml water into a medium pan and bring to the boil over a high heat. Add the fish balls and cook for 10 minutes, stirring from time to time to prevent them from sticking together. Drain.
5 Clean the pan, pour in the chicken stock and bring to the boil over a high heat. Drop in the cooked fish balls and pak choi leaves and cook for a further 4–5 minutes, then add the sesame oil.
6 To serve, spoon six fish balls into each soup bowl, divide the pak choi leaves evenly and pour over the hot broth.

 LISA'S TIP As a substitute for fresh, you can use frozen fish fillets in the mixture instead. Simply defrost the fish fillets and drain the liquid. Blend in the same way as in the instructions above.

Fish & Mango Wontons

When I was a child my father would swing me around in his arms as if I was as light as a feather. And if I was good he would sometimes reward me with a mango. He taught me how to cut one side first and turn it into a hedgehog so that it was easier to eat, and then cut the other side into a hedgehog – while he sucked on the middle bit, which was essentially the central large stone. I absolutely loved the flavour of those mangoes – they were sweet and juicy – and I savoured those moments I spent with him. This dim sum is dedicated to our father, who loves fish and mango. The flavour is unique because it imparts a sweet and fresh element from the mango and a savoury taste from the fish, but it is a delicious combination.

MAKES **12**
PREPARATION TIME **30 minutes, plus 15 minutes resting time**
COOKING TIME **20 minutes**

400g white fish, such as haddock, sea bass, cod or halibut
2 mangoes, cut into 2cm dice
2cm piece of fresh root ginger, finely chopped
1 teaspoon salt
1 teaspoon caster sugar
1 teaspoon white pepper
1 tablespoon Shaoxing wine
1 tablespoon light soy sauce
1 teaspoon sesame oil
1 tablespoon potato starch
12 wonton pastry wrappers
200ml vegetable oil, for deep-frying
Sweet and Sour Sauce (see page 156), to serve

1 First make the filling. Put the fish in a food processor and blitz to a smooth paste. Transfer to a bowl and add the chopped mango, ginger, salt, sugar, pepper, Shaoxing wine, light soy sauce, sesame oil and potato starch. Using a wooden spoon, mix the ingredients in a clockwise motion until they come together into a sticky paste. Cover the bowl with clingfilm and transfer the mixture to the fridge to rest for 15 minutes.
2 To assemble the wontons, scoop 1 heaped tablespoon of the filling into the centre of each wonton wrapper – don't overfill. Wet the edges of the pastry and turn into a triangle shape. Push the triangle ends to the centre of the wonton, making a pointy shape resembling a bishop's hat. Use a dab of water to seal the pastry edges. Repeat with the rest of the pastry and filling to form 12 wontons all together.
3 Preheat the vegetable oil to 180°C in a wok over a high heat (to test the temperature, see page 149). Lower the dumplings carefully into the hot oil and cook for 5–6 minutes, flipping them over until both sides are golden brown. Serve with Sweet and Sour Sauce.

 LISA'S TIP These wontons can be made up in advance and frozen. They can then be fried straight from frozen; cook for a further 5 minutes to ensure the filling is cooked through.

Prawn, Quinoa & Kidney Bean Dumplings

蝦藜和芸豆水晶餃

Kidney beans are no-one's kidneys but actually a legume. They are just shaped like a kidney, which is why that name has stuck. Once cooked, kidney beans are quite tasty and full of iron, protein, zinc and fibre, which helps to keep you strong and give you energy. I make this dim sum for students at our cookery school and they always ask about the name.

MAKES **12**

PREPARATION TIME **1 hour, plus 20 minutes resting time**

COOKING TIME **10 minutes**

85g quinoa

150g raw, peeled king prawns, deveined

50g green beans, finely diced

1 small carrot, finely diced

50g peas

10 pistachio nuts, roughly chopped

50g cooked red kidney beans

1 teaspoon light soy sauce

1 teaspoon caster sugar

1 teaspoon salt

¼ teaspoon white pepper

1 teaspoon Shaoxing rice wine

1 teaspoon sesame oil

2cm piece of fresh root ginger, finely chopped

1 tablespoon potato starch

For the dumpling wrappers

120g wheat starch

70g tapioca flour, plus extra for dusting

1 teaspoon salt

2 teaspoons vegetable oil

180–200ml boiling water

sriracha hot sauce or soy sauce, to serve

1 To cook the quinoa, heat 250ml water in a medium saucepan over a medium heat until it comes to the boil. Add the quinoa and stir. Bring back to the boil, then reduce the heat to low and simmer, covered, until the quinoa absorbs the water, approx. 20 minutes. Remove from the heat and set aside for 10 minutes, still covered.

2 Rinse the king prawns under cold running water and pat dry on kitchen paper. Slice each king prawn into four pieces, and then flatten each piece with a large knife or hammer until it is 5mm thick. Transfer the prawns to a bowl.

3 Add the quinoa, green beans, carrot, peas, pistachios and kidney beans and mix well. Season with the light soy sauce, sugar, salt, white pepper, Shaoxing wine, sesame oil, ginger and potato starch. Mix in a clockwise direction until thoroughly combined, then cover the bowl with clingfilm and transfer the filling to the fridge to rest for 15 minutes while you prepare the dumpling wrappers.

4 To make the dumpling wrappers, combine the wheat starch and tapioca flour in a bowl with the salt and oil. Mix together in a clockwise direction with a wooden spoon, then gradually add enough boiling water so that the dough comes together in a ball. Use your hand to knead the dough until smooth. Cover the bowl with a damp cloth and set aside to rest at room temperature for 20 minutes.

5 Turn out the dough onto a floured work surface and knead with your hands until smooth, approx. 5 minutes. Roll into an 18cm log and cut into 12 even pieces. Flatten each piece with the palm of your hand and use a rolling pin to roll it into an even circle, approx. 6cm in diameter.

6 To assemble the dumplings, place 1 heaped tablespoon of filling in the centre of each wrapper. Fold over one-third of the pastry into a half-moon shape and pinch the edges to seal that side. To create the triangular shape and two corners, push the middle of the pastry to the centre and then crimp the edges together. This will create two distinctive corners. Mould the dumpling into a triangular shape by further crimping the edges to seal the pastry. Arrange the dumplings spaced 1cm apart inside a bamboo steamer lined with baking parchment.

7 To cook the dumplings, fill a wok with water so that it is just over one-quarter full. Set a round cake rack in the centre, cover with a lid and bring to the boil over a high heat. Place the bamboo steamer inside the wok and steam for 10 minutes. Remove from the heat and leave the lid of the steamer slightly ajar to allow some steam to escape for 2 minutes. Serve hot with sriracha hot sauce or soy sauce.

Prawn Dumplings
蝦餃

This famous Har Gow dumpling, which comprises a prawn filling wrapped in a delicate, pearly white dumpling skin, is said to be the one that the skill of a dim sum chef is judged on. At the Sweet Mandarin Cookery School we've had competitions to see how many pleats one can imprint. Although you could go for a respectable five pleats, to really show flair you should aim for seven upwards. Pleating the dumplings is quite tricky as the delicate skins split if they are overhandled – this results in a broken dumpling, the cardinal sin of this particular dim sum. This pastry cannot be made in advance and chilled or it will split when rolled out. Therefore only make enough pastry as you need.

MAKES **12**
PREPARATION TIME **40 minutes, plus**
20 minutes resting time
COOKING TIME **10 minutes**

250g raw, peeled king prawns,
   deveined
225g bamboo shoots, cut into 5mm
   dice
1cm piece of fresh root ginger, grated
1½ teaspoons salt
1½ teaspoons caster sugar
½ teaspoon white pepper
1 teaspoon sesame oil
1 egg white
2 tablespoons potato starch
1 tablespoon water
For the dumpling wrappers
120g wheat starch
70g tapioca flour, plus extra
   for dusting
1 teaspoon salt
2 teaspoons vegetable oil
180–200ml boiling water
sriracha hot sauce or soy sauce,
   to serve

1 Wash the king prawns under cold running water and pat dry on kitchen paper. Chop each prawn into 4 pieces, and then flatten each piece using a large knife or hammer until it is 5mm thick.

2 Combine the prawns in a bowl with the bamboo shoots, ginger, salt, sugar, pepper, sesame oil, egg white and potato starch and water. Mix the ingredients in a clockwise direction using a wooden spoon until they come together in a sticky paste. Cover the bowl with clingfilm and transfer the filling to the fridge for 15 minutes.

3 To make the dumpling wrappers, put the wheat starch and tapioca flour in a medium bowl and add the salt and oil. Mix together in a clockwise direction with a wooden spoon, and then gradually add enough boiling water so that the dough comes together in a ball. Use your hand to knead the dough until smooth. Cover the bowl with a damp cloth and set aside to rest at room temperature for 20 minutes.

4 Turn out the dough onto a floured work surface and knead. Roll into a log, approx. 18cm long. Cut into 12 even pieces. Flatten each piece with the palm of your hand, and then roll out to a circle approx. 6cm in diameter.

5 To assemble the dumplings, place 1 heaped tablespoon of filling in the centre of each circle and begin to pleat one side (the furthest side) of the wrapper. Firstly fold over the pastry into a half-moon shape and then pinch the corner end on the right-hand side of the dumpling to close and start pleating there. Using your left-hand index finger, crease one to two folds to the right to give it the pleated effect. Continue with the folds until the furthest side of the pastry is all pleated. You may find the filling being pushed out of the dumpling; if so, use the left-hand thumb to push the filling back in. Then, using the right-hand thumb and index finger, crimp the edge of the pastry to fully close the dumpling. The right-hand thumb can be used to shape the back of the dumpling into a moon-shaped curve. Arrange the dumplings inside a bamboo steamer lined with baking parchment.

6 To cook the dumplings, fill a wok with water so that it is just over one-quarter full. Set a round cake rack in the centre, cover with a lid and bring to the boil over a high heat. Place the bamboo steamer inside the wok and steam the dumplings for 10 minutes. Remove from the heat and leave the lid of the steamer slightly ajar to allow some steam to escape for 2 minutes. Serve hot with sriracha hot sauce or soy sauce.

Water Chestnut & Prawn Dumplings

潮州粉粿

This dim sum originates from Chiu Chow in the Guangdong Province, a place famous for its opera, music, Kung Fu tea (the espresso of tea) and these wonderful dumplings. Just like the city, there is flair in these dumplings, which pack contrasting colours, flavours and textures together in one single mouthful. They say that opposites attract. In the midst of this oozy gelatinous dim sum, there is a crunch of water chestnuts and the contrast really works. If you want to include another filling, other suggested ingredients include cashew nuts, shallots, chicken and pork.

MAKES **12**

PREPARATION TIME **50 minutes – 1 hour,** **plus 10 minutes soaking and 35 minutes resting time**

COOKING TIME **10 minutes**

12 dried Chinese mushrooms

500g raw, peeled king prawns, deveined

225g water chestnuts, finely diced

1 medium carrot, finely diced

1 tablespoon light soy sauce

1 teaspoon caster sugar

1 teaspoon salt

¼ teaspoon white pepper

1 tablespoon Shaoxing rice wine

1 teaspoon sesame oil

1cm piece of fresh root ginger, finely chopped

1 teaspoon potato starch

For the dumpling wrappers

120g wheat starch, plus extra for dusting

70g tapioca flour, plus extra for dusting

1 teaspoon salt

2 teaspoons vegetable oil

180–200ml boiling water

sriracha hot sauce or soy sauce, to serve

1 Place the Chinese mushrooms in a small bowl, cover with hot water and set aside to soak for 10 minutes; drain well, discarding the soaking liquor, and cut into fine dice. Cut each prawn into 4 pieces, and then flatten each piece with a knife or hammer until it is 5mm thick. Combine the prawns, water chestnuts, mushrooms and carrot in a bowl. Season with soy sauce, sugar, salt, white pepper, Shaoxing wine, sesame oil, ginger and potato starch. Mix the ingredients together in a clockwise direction using a wooden spoon until thoroughly combined. Cover the bowl with clingfilm and transfer the filling to the fridge to rest for 15 minutes.

2 To make the dumpling wrappers, combine the wheat starch and tapioca flour in a bowl with the salt and oil. Mix together in a clockwise direction with a wooden spoon, and then gradually add enough boiling water so that the dough comes together in a ball. It will be bright white in colour, like snow. Use your hand to knead the dough until smooth. Cover the bowl with a damp cloth and set aside to rest at room temperature for 20 minutes.

3 Turn out the dough onto a floured work surface and knead with your hands until smooth, approx. 5 minutes. Roll into an 18cm log and cut into 12 even pieces. Flatten each piece with the palm of your hand and use a rolling pin to roll it into an even circle, approx. 6cm in diameter.

4 To assemble the dumplings, place 1 heaped tablespoon of the filling in the centre of each wrapper. Wet the edges, fold in half to enclose the filling and then sit the dumpling up so that it looks like a half moon with a flat bottom. Crimp the edges into a wavy shape using your thumb and index finger. Place the completed dumplings inside a bamboo steamer lined with baking parchment, leaving a gap of 1cm between each one to prevent them from sticking together.

5 To cook the dumplings, fill a wok with water so that it is just over one-quarter full. Set a round cake rack in the centre, cover with a lid and bring to the boil over a high heat. Place the bamboo steamer inside the wok and steam for 10 minutes. Remove from the heat and leave the lid of the steamer slightly ajar to allow some steam to escape for 2 minutes. Serve hot with sriracha hot sauce or soy sauce.

Mushroom, Prawn & Edamame Dumplings

招牌蝦餃

Our grandmother, Lily Kwok, would add as much coriander as she possibly could to dishes because she said she felt better after eating it. But she had a point: scientific research has shown that coriander lowers blood sugar levels and generates the production of insulin. It is also anti-inflammatory and antibacterial. Coriander has a lovely pungent smell, which lifts this dumpling to another level.

MAKES **12**
PREPARATION TIME **40 minutes, plus
20 minutes resting time**
COOKING TIME **10 minutes**

2 tablespoons edamame beans
**250g raw, peeled king prawns,
   deveined**
**10 shiitake mushrooms, finely
   chopped**
3 tablespoons finely chopped chives
**5mm piece of fresh root ginger,
   finely chopped**
1 sprig of coriander, roughly chopped
1 teaspoon salt
1 teaspoon caster sugar
¼ teaspoon white pepper
½ teaspoon sesame oil
1 teaspoon potato starch
For the dumpling wrappers
120g wheat starch
**70g tapioca flour, plus extra
   for dusting**
1 teaspoon salt
2 teaspoons vegetable oil
180–200ml boiling water
**sriracha hot sauce or soy sauce,
   to serve**

1 Cook the edamame beans for 8–10 minutes in a pan of salted boiling water. Meanwhile, rinse the king prawns under cold running water and pat dry on kitchen paper. Slice each king prawn into 4 pieces, and then flatten each piece with a large knife or hammer until it is 5mm thick. Transfer the prawns to a bowl.

2 Add the edamame beans, mushrooms, chives, ginger and coriander. Season with salt, sugar, pepper, sesame oil and potato starch. Mix the filling in a clockwise direction using a wooden spoon until it comes together in a sticky paste. Cover the bowl with clingfilm and transfer the filling to the fridge to rest for 15 minutes.

3 To make the dumpling wrappers, combine the wheat starch and tapioca flour in a bowl with the salt and oil. Mix together in a clockwise direction with a wooden spoon, and then gradually add enough boiling water so that the dough comes together in a ball. It will be bright white in colour, like snow. Use your hand to knead the dough until smooth. Cover the bowl with a damp cloth and set aside to rest at room temperature for 20 minutes.

4 Turn out the dough onto a floured work surface, knead and roll into an 18cm log. Cut into 12 even-sized pieces. Flatten each piece with the palm of the hand, and then roll out to a circle approx. 6cm in diameter using a rolling pin.

5 To assemble the dumplings, place 1 heaped tablespoon of filling in the centre of each circle and begin to pleat one side (the furthest side) of the wrapper. Firstly fold over the pastry into a half-moon shape and then pinch the corner end on the right-hand side of the dumpling to close and start pleating there. Using your left-hand index finger, crease one to two folds to the right to give it the pleated effect. Continue with the folds until the furthest side of the pastry is all pleated. You may find the filling being pushed out of the dumpling; if so, use the left-hand thumb to push the filling back in. Then, using the right-hand thumb and index finger, crimp the edge of the pastry to fully close the dumpling. The right-hand thumb can be used to shape the back of the dumpling into a moon-shaped curve. Arrange the dumplings inside a bamboo steamer lined with baking parchment.

6 To cook the dumplings, fill a wok with water so that it is just over one-quarter full. Set a round cake rack in the centre, cover with a lid and bring to the boil over a high heat. Place the bamboo steamer inside the wok and steam the dumplings for 10 minutes. Remove from the heat and leave the lid of the steamer slightly ajar to allow some steam to escape for 2 minutes. Serve hot with sriracha hot sauce or soy sauce.

Crispy Prawn & Chive Parcels
香脆的蝦和韭菜春捲

When I close my eyes I can still picture the sunlight streaming into the kitchen, creating light strobes as it hit the chive flowers on the windowsill. The chives had long green stalks with beautiful purple flowers at the end, and my grandmother would often pluck one and put it in my hair. She whipped the chives from her makeshift herb garden and I watched her in awe as she transformed them into these crispy delights with a steamed centre. These parcels can be made in advance and placed in the freezer, then deep-fried from frozen, but they will need a further 5 minutes to cook until they are hot inside. To ensure the filling is cooked completely, slice one in half and check the filling is hot. If it is not at the right temperature, cook it for a further 2–3 minutes over a lower heat to prevent the pastry from browning too fast.

MAKES **20**

PREPARATION TIME **15 minutes, plus**
15 minutes resting and 30 minutes
chilling time

COOKING TIME **5 minutes**

250g raw, peeled king prawns,
  deveined
25g chives, finely chopped
1 teaspoon salt
1 teaspoon caster sugar
1 teaspoon sesame oil
1cm piece of fresh root ginger,
  finely chopped
2 teaspoons Shaoxing rice wine
1 tablespoon potato starch
10 spring roll pastry wrappers,
  approx. 8cm square, halved into
  triangles
1 tablespoon plain flour mixed with
  2 tablespoons water to form a paste
vegetable oil, for deep-frying
Sweet and Sour Sauce (see page 156),
  to serve

1 Rinse the king prawns under cold running water and pat dry on kitchen paper. Slice each king prawn into 4 pieces, and then flatten each piece with a large knife or hammer until it is 5mm thick. Transfer the prawns to a bowl.

2 Add the chives, salt, sugar, sesame oil, ginger, Shaoxing wine and potato starch. Mix the filling in a clockwise direction using a wooden spoon until it comes together in a sticky paste. Cover the bowl with clingfilm and transfer the filling to the fridge to rest for 15 minutes while you make the pastry.

3 To assemble the parcels, lay out a spring roll wrapper on a work surface with the tip of the triangle facing you. Brush the edges facing you with flour-and-water paste and place 2 tablespoons of filling in the centre, leaving a border around the outside. Roll the wrapper away from you until the tip of the triangle meets the edge. Brush with flour-and-water paste to seal. Brush the centre of the rolled parcel with flour-and-water paste and fold in the sides to seal.

4 Repeat with the remaining wrappers to make 10 parcels altogether. Arrange the parcels on a baking tray and transfer them to the freezer to firm up for approx. 30 minutes.

5 Remove the parcels from the freezer. Fill a wok one-quarter full with vegetable oil and preheat to 180°C (to test the temperature, see page 149). Carefully lower the prawn parcels into the hot oil and cook for 5–6 minutes, flipping them over occasionally until they are golden brown on both sides. Drain on kitchen paper, cut in half and serve with Sweet and Sour Sauce.

Crispy Prawn Dumplings
明蝦餃

This recipe for Ming Har Gok was inspired by opening the fridge and using leftovers to make dumplings. What really helps to bind the filling together is the kale, which is what Chinese restaurants fry to make crispy seaweed. When it is not fried, kale has the texture and taste of cabbage but fired up with extra nutrients and minerals. The leaves are dark in colour, and in a salad they can be hard to eat, almost rubbery and not very tasty. But when cooked, kale softens, sweetens and becomes a superfood in its own right. It is packed with vitamin C and antioxidants, which help to protect the immune system and lower LDL cholesterol. It's great in this dim sum as it retains its sweetness against the other flavours competing for attention and it does not sweat as much as cabbage, so the dim sum doesn't become soggy.

MAKES **12**
PREPARATION TIME **20 minutes**
COOKING TIME **12 minutes**

150g quinoa
150g raw, peeled king prawns, deveined
2cm piece of fresh root ginger, finely chopped
2 medium tomatoes, diced
100g kale, shredded
1 ripe avocado, diced
1 teaspoon salt
1 teaspoon sugar
1 teaspoon white pepper
1 teaspoon sesame oil
1 tablespoon light soy sauce
1 tablespoon potato starch
12 wonton wrappers (made for deep-frying)
200ml vegetable oil, for deep-frying
salad cream, to serve

1 Rinse the quinoa under cold water and fill a medium saucepan with boiling water. Add the quinoa and cook for 20 minutes over a medium heat until it has fully absorbed the water. Remove from the heat and leave to cool.

2 Wash and then soak the king prawns in damp kitchen paper. Chop each prawn into 4 pieces then flatten each piece using a large knife or hammer until it is 5mm thick.

3 Transfer the prawns to a bowl and add the ginger, tomatoes, kale and avocado. Then add the cooked quinoa. Season with salt, sugar, pepper, sesame oil, light soy sauce and potato starch. Mix the filling in a clockwise direction until it all sticks together.

4 Scoop 1 tablespoon of filling into the centre of each wonton wrapper. Wet the edge of the wrappers and close to form a triangle. Once the edge of the triangle is closed, dab some water in the middle of the slope on the left and right of the triangle. Fold up the edge of the pastry so that it's pleating back on itself. Then crimp it so that it moulds in place.

5 Heat the vegetable oil in a wok over a high heat and when it's almost smoking drop the dumplings carefully into the oil and cook for 5–6 minutes, turning until all the sides are golden brown. Serve with salad cream for dipping.

 LISA'S TIP When making these dumplings make sure that the edges are completely sealed to prevent them bursting open during cooking.

Crispy Prawn Balls
炸蝦球

Our grandmother told me that this dish symbolises the beauty and pain of women who have had their feet bound. It was believed in archaic Chinese culture that a woman's beauty was judged by how small her feet were and therefore young girls would have their feet crushed into bits and bound up as the fractures bled. As compensation, these crispy prawn balls were made to appease the distressed child.

MAKES **12**
PREPARATION TIME **15 minutes, plus**
30 minutes chilling time
COOKING TIME **20 minutes**

300g raw, peeled king prawns,
   deveined
150g white fish fillet, such as cod,
   haddock, hake, sea bass or halibut
2 spring onions, finely sliced
2 egg whites
1 teaspoon crushed garlic
1cm piece of fresh root ginger,
   finely chopped
1 teaspoon salt
1 teaspoon caster sugar
2 tablespoons Shaoxing rice wine
2 tablespoons potato starch
1 teaspoon sesame oil
300ml vegetable oil, for deep-frying
Sweet Chilli Sauce (see page 156),
   to serve

1 To make the filling, put the raw prawns and fish in a food processor. Add the spring onions, egg whites, garlic, ginger, salt, sugar, Shaoxing wine, potato starch and sesame oil. Blitz for 5 minutes until the mixture resembles a smooth paste. Scrape out the mixture into a bowl, cover with clingfilm and transfer to the fridge to firm up for 30 minutes.

2 Using a melon baller, scoop out spoonfuls of the filling and shape into 12 firm balls in your hands. Place the finished balls on a plate.

3 Preheat the oil to 180°C in a wok or deep saucepan over a high heat (to check the temperature, see page 149). Carefully lower the prawn balls into the hot oil – initially they will drop to the bottom and then float back up to the surface. Use a slotted spoon to move the prawn balls around in the hot fat to stop them from sticking together. Cook for 7–8 minutes until golden brown all over. Remove the prawn balls from the pan and drain on kitchen paper. Serve with Sweet Chilli Sauce.

Deep-fried Prawns in Bean Curd Sheets

香炸鮮蝦腐皮卷

This recipe was created after I stumbled back to Sweet Mandarin still hungry from a party where I had been too nervous to eat anything. There was some wasabi left and I decided to grab that and mix it with mayonnaise to temper the inevitable kick. An additional order of deep-fried prawns in bean curd sheets had been made up and I hungrily tucked into them with my new wasabi mayo. The wasabi hit was exactly what I needed. Wasabi's heat is more akin to hot mustard than the capsaicin in chilli pepper, producing vapours that stimulate the nasal passages more than the tongue. The plant grows naturally along stream beds in mountain river valleys in Japan, but has proved very popular in modern Chinese cuisine.

MAKES **12**
PREPARATION TIME **20 minutes**
COOKING TIME **15 minutes**

12 bean curd sheets, approx. 8cm
    square
500g raw, peeled king prawns,
    deveined
1 spring onion, finely sliced
1 teaspoon salt
1 teaspoon caster sugar
1 tablespoon Shaoxing rice wine
1 teaspoon sesame oil
1 teaspoon potato starch
200ml vegetable oil, for deep-frying
rocket, to serve
For the wasabi mayonnaise
2 teaspoons wasabi paste
120g ready-made mayonnaise
2 tablespoons fresh lemon juice

1 When you buy the beancurd sheets they come in one very large sheet. You will need to portion them out to make the wrappers.

2 Rinse the king prawns under cold running water and pat dry on kitchen paper. Slice each king prawn into 4 pieces, and then flatten each piece with a large knife or hammer until it is 5mm thick. Transfer the prawns to a bowl.

3 Add the spring onion, salt, sugar, Shaoxing wine, sesame oil and potato starch. Mix the ingredients together in a clockwise direction for 3 minutes until the mixture comes together in a sticky paste.

4 To assemble the parcels, position a bean curd sheet on a work surface so one edge is parallel to the edge of the work surface. Place 1 tablespoon of the filling at the base, closest to you, and fold the beancurd sheet over to enclose the filling. Bring the left-hand side over the filling, followed by the right-hand side, and then roll up tightly to form a spring roll shape. Seal the overlap with a cocktail stick. Repeat with the remaining sheets and filling to form 12 parcels altogether.

5 To cook the bean curd parcels, fill a wok half full with vegetable oil and preheat to 180°C over a high heat (to test the temperature, see page 149). Lower the bean curd parcels into the hot oil and cook for 6–7 minutes, turning occasionally. (You may have to do this in batches.) Drain on kitchen paper.

6 Meanwhile, prepare the wasabi mayonnaise by mixing all the ingredients together in a small bowl. Serve on a bed of fresh rocket with the wasabi mayonnaise drizzled over the finished dish.

 LISA'S TIP Bean curd sheets need to be covered with a clean cloth to prevent them drying out. They are very brittle, so roll them just like a spring roll.

Sesame Prawn Toasts
芝麻蝦多士

I remember sesame seeds being thrown at a Chinese wedding as a symbol of fertility. The bride wasn't amused, as the seeds became a semi-permanent fixture in her hair (even visible in the wedding photos) and some even went down her dress. In this recipe the key to creating the perfect golden crust is to use untoasted sesame seeds.

MAKES **16 triangles**
PREPARATION TIME **10 minutes, plus
40 minutes chilling time**
COOKING TIME **25 minutes**

**4 medium slices of good-quality
   white bread, crusts removed
500g raw, peeled king prawns,
   deveined
2 egg whites
2 tablespoons Shaoxing rice wine
1 teaspoon salt
1 teaspoon caster sugar
¼ teaspoon white pepper
1 teaspoon sesame oil
200g untoasted sesame seeds
500ml vegetable oil, for deep-frying
Sweet and Sour Sauce (see page 156),
   to serve**

1 Put the slices of bread in the freezer for approx. 20 minutes until they harden up. Meanwhile, make the prawn paste. Combine the king prawns, egg whites, Shaoxing wine, salt, sugar and pepper in a food processor and blitz to a smooth paste. Add the sesame oil and blitz briefly to combine.

2 Remove the bread from the freezer and, using a butter knife, spread a layer of prawn paste onto each slice. Make sure you get it right into the corners and don't spread it too thinly – it needs to be approx. 3mm thick all over.

3 Tip the sesame seeds onto a plate and press the bread into the sesame seeds, paste-side down. Make sure each slice is really well covered with seeds, right into the corners. Arrange the slices of sesame-coated prawn bread on a baking tray and transfer them to the freezer to firm up for 20 minutes.

4 Preheat the vegetable oil to 180°C in a wok or deep saucepan (to check the temperature, see page 149). Cut each slice of prawn bread into four triangles and lower them into the hot oil, seed-side down. Cook for 5–6 minutes until golden brown all over, flipping them halfway through the cooking time. Cook the prawn toasts in batches to ensure they all cook evenly and to prevent the pan from overcrowding. Drain on kitchen paper and serve with Sweet and Sour Sauce.

 LISA'S TIP The spread can be made in advance and stored in the fridge until needed. Alternatively, you could freeze the sesame-coated prawn bread in its raw state and deep-fry it straight from the freezer.

Mango & Prawn Rolls

芒果鮮蝦卷

Legend has it that thousands of years ago Buddha was presented with a mango grove so that he could rest in the shade, and since then mangos have been cultivated in north-east India, Myanmar and Bangladesh. Their sweet, juicy flesh pairs perfectly with succulent king prawns.

MAKES **15**

PREPARATION TIME **20 minutes, plus**
15 minutes chilling time

COOKING TIME **25 minutes**

150g raw, peeled king prawns,
   deveined

150g mango flesh, cut into 1cm dice

150g tinned mango, cut into 1cm dice

2cm piece of fresh root ginger,
   finely chopped

1 teaspoon salt

1 teaspoon caster sugar

½ teaspoon white pepper

1 tablespoon light soy sauce

1 teaspoon sesame oil

2 tablespoons potato starch

15 spring roll pastry wrappers (made
   for deep-frying), approx. 8cm
   square

1 tablespoon plain flour and
   1 tablespoon water, mixed together
   to form a paste

vegetable oil, for deep-frying

mayonnaise, to serve

1 Rinse the king prawns under cold running water and pat dry on kitchen paper. Slice each king prawn into 4 pieces, and then flatten each piece with a large knife or hammer until it is 5mm thick. Transfer the prawns to a bowl.

2 Add the chopped mango, ginger, salt, sugar, pepper, light soy sauce, sesame oil and potato starch and mix the filling in a clockwise direction for 3 minutes until the ingredients come together in a sticky paste. Cover the bowl with clingfilm and transfer the filling to the fridge to rest for 15 minutes.

3 Separate the spring roll wrappers and start with the first sheet. Open up the sheet and turn it so that one corner is facing you, like a diamond. Place 1 heaped tablespoon of the filling in the corner closest to you. Bring the corner over the filling to enclose it and roll forward, stopping at the middle. Brush a little flour-and-water paste on the remaining corners using a pastry brush. Fold the left corner over the filling, followed by the right corner, and then roll up tightly to seal the spring roll. Repeat with the rest of the mixture to form 15 spring rolls in total.

4 To cook the spring rolls, fill a wok half full with vegetable oil and preheat over a high heat to 180°C (to test the temperature, see page 149). Lower the spring rolls into the hot oil and cook for 6–7 minutes or until golden, turning constantly. Cook in batches of 5 to prevent overcrowding the pan. Serve with mayonnaise.

 LISA'S TIP Make sure you drain all the liquid from the mangos before adding to the mixture. It's essential that there is no liquid in the filling otherwise the spring rolls will burst when cooking.

Pan-seared Scallops with Black Truffle

香煎扇貝配黑松露和辣椒油

This is a simple yet amazingly delicious combination – perfect for a special occasion alongside a glass of Champagne. I created this dish while working as a VIP chef. The VIPs loved black truffles and nicknamed them 'black diamonds', so I created a dim sum using them, pairing the truffle with scallops. They look stunning together and the woody intensity of the truffle pairs perfectly with the delicate flavour of the scallops. This is my take on the steamed scallop with ginger and spring onion. Scallops can be very diverse and pairing them with unusual ingredients such as truffles and sesame oil can really be an amazing combination on the palate. Scallops are characterised by having two types of meat in one shell: the adductor muscle, called the scallop, which is white and meaty, and the roe, called the coral, which is red or white and soft. This recipe works with both the scallop and the coral.

SERVES **2**
PREPARATION TIME **10 minutes**
COOKING TIME **5 minutes**

2 black truffles
½ teaspoon sesame oil
1 teaspoon sea salt
1 tablespoon vegetable oil
6 jumbo scallops
6 clean scallop shells (optional),
  to serve

1 Make the garnish by wiping down the black truffles. Finely dice the truffles and transfer to a bowl. Stir in the sesame oil and sea salt and set aside.
2 Heat a wok over a medium heat and add the vegetable oil. Sear the jumbo scallops on both sides until golden brown, approx. 4 minutes. Serve, garnished with the black truffle, on scallop shells or serving plates.

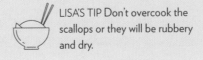
LISA'S TIP Don't overcook the scallops or they will be rubbery and dry.

Pan-Fried Prawn Cakes

香煎蝦餅

My family returned to Hong Kong only once during my childhood to attend a family wedding. The sun in Hong Kong was scorching my plaits that day, but it didn't deter me from playing with the other children. I chased after a little boy about the same age as me, laughing and calling out to him in Cantonese to slow down. We ran all the way down to the beach at Stanley Market, where the dai pai dong vendors were selling these amazing pan-fried shrimp cakes. The boy only had enough money for one portion, but he was kind enough to share his with me. In return I gave him a peck on the cheek. He blushed from ear to ear, redder than the sweet chilli sauce that accompanied those tasty treats!

MAKES **6**
PREPARATION TIME **20 minutes**
COOKING TIME **12 minutes**

80g green beans
200g raw, peeled king prawns,
    deveined
1 shallot, finely diced
1 garlic clove, finely diced
2cm piece of fresh root ginger,
    finely chopped
½ spring onion, finely sliced
½ teaspoon salt
1 teaspoon caster sugar
pinch of white pepper
1 teaspoon sesame oil
1 teaspoon potato starch
2 tablespoons vegetable oil, plus
    extra for greasing
Sweet Chilli Sauce (see page 156),
    to serve

1 Wash the green beans, pat dry on kitchen paper and cut into small pieces.
2 Rinse the king prawns under cold running water and pat dry on kitchen paper. Slice each king prawn into 4 pieces, and then flatten each piece with a large knife or hammer until it is 5mm thick. Transfer the prawns to a bowl.
3 Add the shallot, garlic, ginger, spring onion and green beans. Season with the salt, sugar, pepper, sesame oil and potato starch and mix the ingredients together in a clockwise direction for 3 minutes until they come together in a sticky paste.
4 Divide the mixture into 6 even portions. Grease the palms of your hands with a little oil and shape the mixture into balls. Arrange on a plate.
5 Heat a wok over a high heat with the oil. Drop the prawn balls into the hot oil and press them down with a flat spatula to form a patty shape. Cook for 3 minutes on each side until golden brown. (You may have to do this in batches.) Serve with Sweet Chilli Sauce.

 LISA'S TIP To ensure the prawn patties are fully cooked, insert a skewer into the centre and if it comes out clean they are ready.

Boiled Wonton Soup
上湯雲吞

When I was 11 years old, I went to Singapore to meet my great aunt who lived there. The first thing that hit me was the heat which felt hotter than its 35°C because of the humidity. My great aunty sensed that I wasn't feeling well because of the extreme heat outside and the cold air-conditioning inside. She ushered me to a makeshift vendor cart on the back of a tricycle, which opened up to reveal a gas canister under the seat for heating up a soup pot. I could smell the goodness of the soup, which was bubbling away with wontons floating on the top. She explained to me that this was the perfect soup when one felt under the weather and that the translation of 'wonton' means 'to swallow a cloud'. If you have a sore throat, this is the perfect soup, because the wonton dumplings are easy to swallow. The vendor poured the hot soup into a plastic transparent bag and threw in the dumplings and a sprinkling of spring onions. Then he tied the top with a knot and an elastic band. Both bags of soup were then put into another bag that he gave to me. My great aunt laughed, because my mouth was wide open in shock that this guy had just served up soup in a bag. When we got home, great aunty snipped a corner of the bag and poured out the soup into a bowl, then she tipped the wonton dumplings and spring onions into the bowl and gave it to me. I remember slurping up that soup noisily – apparently this is a sign to show appreciation of the dish, but also it was because I was hungry and it was delicious. The dumplings were a real treat – meaty and flavourful – and they helped me to feel better with every mouthful.

MAKES **12**
PREPARATION TIME **15 minutes, plus**
50 minutes chilling time
COOKING TIME **14 minutes**

400g raw, peeled king prawns,
 deveined
1 egg, beaten
2 teaspoons light soy sauce
1 teaspoon salt
1 teaspoon caster sugar
1 teaspoon sesame oil
1 tablespoon potato starch
12 wonton wrappers
500ml chicken stock
5 pak choi, leaves separated and
 roughly chopped
1 spring onion, finely diced

1 Combine the king prawns, egg, 1 teaspoon of the light soy sauce, the salt, sugar, sesame oil and potato starch in a food processor and blitz to a smooth paste. Cover the bowl with clingfilm and transfer to the fridge to rest for 40 minutes.

2 To assemble the dumplings, peel off a wonton wrapper and place $1/2$ tablespoon of the prawn mixture in the centre. Dab the edges with water and fold in half to form a little triangular parcel. crimp the sides so that it folds towards the centre. Arrange the finished wontons on a baking tray and transfer them to the freezer to firm up for 10 minutes.

3 Meanwhile, fill a medium saucepan with water and bring to the boil. Lower the wontons into the boiling water and cook for 7 minutes, stirring occasionally to stop them from sticking together. Drain well.

4 Heat the chicken stock in a separate pan over a high heat and season with the remaining light soy sauce. Add the cooked wonton dumplings to the boiling chicken stock and cook for a further 5 minutes.

5 Add the pak choi and cook for a further 2 minutes.

6 To serve, ladle the pak choi and dumplings evenly into 4 bowls. Pour over the chicken stock and scatter over the chopped spring onion.

 LISA'S TIP You can freeze the wontons once they are made and use a portion at a time to make the soup. They are perfect for a light supper or when you get home late after work.

Jee Cheung Fun
腸粉

This dim sum's Chinese name, Jee Cheung Fun, is quite a strange one: translated literally it means 'pig intestine noodles'. I can reassure you there is no pig intestine in this dish; the reason it is called that is because the rice roll is rolled over and over again until it resembles the small intestine of a pig. This dish could also be made with beef, king prawns, scallops or Char Siu. Just make sure you steam the raw ingredients first, for approx. 4 minutes, before sprinkling them over the rice flour mixture in the tray. A non-stick pan would be the perfect utensil for this dish to allow the cooked rice roll to lift off easily.

MAKES **6**
PREPARATION TIME **10 minutes, plus 40 minutes resting time**
COOKING TIME **45 minutes**

230ml water
70g rice flour
½ tablespoon potato starch
1 tablespoon wheat starch
3 tablespoons vegetable oil, plus extra for brushing
¼ teaspoon salt
25g dried shrimps
½ spring onion (green part only), finely sliced, plus extra to garnish
For the sauce
2 teaspoons caster sugar
4 teaspoons warm water
4 teaspoons light soy sauce
2 teaspoons sesame oil

You will need a non-stick roasting tin, approx. 10 x 15cm, that will fit inside your wok

1 Combine the water, rice flour, potato starch, wheat starch, oil and salt in a medium bowl and mix to a smooth paste. Scrape down the sides of the bowl with a spatula, cover the bowl with clingfilm and transfer the mixture to the fridge to rest for 40 minutes.

2 Fill a wok with water so that it is just over one-quarter full. Set a round cake rack in the centre, cover with a lid and bring to the boil over a high heat.

3 Brush a non-stick roasting tin that will fit inside your wok with a little vegetable oil. Add one ladle of the rice flour mixture and tilt the pan from side to side to spread it out in an even layer. Immediately scatter one-sixth of the dried shrimps and some spring onion over the surface.

4 Place the tin inside the wok, resting it on the cake rack, and steam for 7 minutes over a high heat. Carefully remove the tin from the steamer and brush the surface of the rice and prawn sheet with a little oil. Roll it up tightly to form a Swiss roll shape and transfer to a serving plate. Cover with foil to keep warm while you steam the rest of the mixture in the same way to give you 6 rice rolls in total.

5 To make the sauce, combine all the ingredients in a little bowl. Serve the rice rolls with the sauce, garnished with a few spring onions.

 LISA'S TIP As soon as the liquid is poured into the pan, add the filling immediately, as the cooking time for the Cheung Fun is minutes.

Crayfish, Avocado & Red Pepper Wraps

紅椒牛油龍蝦卷

This recipe came about when I was rifling around in the fridge looking for leftovers to turn into something to eat. The addition of the avocado really helps to bind the filling together, although avocados aren't generally used in Chinese cooking. For this version, I have kept true to the ingredients I used when I first created this dish; however, feel free to experiment with your own odds and ends in the fridge and you may be pleasantly surprised. This recipe is a good example of how unusual ingredients can sometimes be paired together with excellent results. The main thing when cooking is to have fun in the kitchen, and I hope you will enjoy making these quick light bites.

MAKES **4**
PREPARATION TIME **20 minutes**
COOKING TIME **5 minutes**

**150ml Sweet Chilli Sauce (see
  page 156)**
2 tablespoons mayonnaise
4 soft tortilla wraps
140g rocket leaves
1 iceberg lettuce, shredded
150g cooked crayfish
2 ripe avocados, sliced
2 tomatoes, thinly sliced
**1 red pepper, deseeded and cut into
  thin strips**

1 Pour the Sweet Chilli Sauce into a small saucepan and cook over a high heat until reduced and thick, approx. 5 minutes. Remove from the heat and stir in the mayonnaise.

2 Spread each wrap with some of the sweet chilli mixture and fill with the rocket, lettuce, crayfish, avocado, tomatoes and red pepper. Roll up the wraps, tucking in the sides so that the filling doesn't escape.

3 Serve cold or hot. To heat, place the wraps on a griddle over a high heat and cook for 3–4 minutes. Slice each completed wrap into 4 pieces to serve.

 LISA'S TIP The trick with the tortilla wrap is similar to the spring roll, you want the wrap to be tightly rolled so that when you slice each wrap the filling does not fall out.

Cuttlefish Dumplings in Spicy Broth

辣湯墨魚餃

Szechuan province is renowned for its chillies, and boasts: 'China is the place for food, Szechuan is the place for flavour.' Szechuan peppercorns and red chillies create that biting, numbing, spicy hotness that many people revel in. They are also the key ingredient in chilli bean paste, which is used to flavour this dish. Dad used to make this broth for Mum in the hope that it would calm down her temper: 'Fight fire with fire', he'd say. This dish is so spicy it also has the effect of keeping her quiet for a bit – until she starts sneezing!

MAKES **24 balls**

PREPARATION TIME **20 minutes, plus 30 minutes chilling time**

COOKING TIME **15 minutes**

300g raw, peeled king prawns, deveined

400g cuttlefish or squid tubes

1 tablespoon egg white

1 teaspoon salt

1 tablespoon tapioca starch

2 tablespoons potato starch, plus more if needed

1 tablespoon vegetable oil

1 teaspoon chilli bean paste

300ml chicken stock

2 bunches of pak choi leaves, quartered

½ teaspoon sesame oil

1 Put the king prawns, cuttlefish or squid, egg white, salt, tapioca and potato starch in a food processor. Pulse until the mixture forms a smooth paste, adding a little water if necessary. (If it's still not combined add more potato starch then proceed with the following throwing technique.)

2 The next step is to make the fish balls' elastic texture. Wet your hands under a cold tap. With a wet hand, scoop up the paste and then throw it back into the bowl. Repeat this process at least 10 times until the paste firms up. Return the filling to the bowl, cover with clingfilm and transfer to the fridge to rest for 30 minutes.

3 Shape the fish mixture into 24 balls, each the size of a grape, in the palms of your hands. Set aside on a plate.

4 Fill a medium saucepan with approx. 300ml water and bring to the boil. Drop in the fish balls and cook for 10 minutes. Drain well.

5 Heat the vegetable oil in a wok over a high heat, add the chilli bean paste and fry for 1 minute. Pour in the chicken stock and stir well to dissolve the chilli bean paste. Bring to the boil over a medium heat. Add the cooked fish balls and the pak choi and cook for 4–5 minutes. Stir in the sesame oil.

6 To serve, divide the fish balls between 4 serving bowls and ladle the stock and pak choi over the top. Serve immediately.

 LISA'S TIP Throwing the balls of fish paste is a traditional Chinese dim sum technique which firms up the mixture. Make sure the fish paste is firm first before throwing.

Fried Squid

炸魷魚

When we were children, Mum told us that squid were very special creatures because they only appeared in the sea when the sky was clear and the universe was calm. At other times they were busy fighting in the sea kingdom against the reef and seaweed enemies, which is what caused the big thrashing waves to crash against the beach and cliffs. We've grown up to look upon this dish as a real treat and love it.

SERVES **2**
PREPARATION TIME **25 minutes**
COOKING TIME **15 minutes**

**2 whole squid, body and tentacles,
cleaned (ink sack and hard cartilage
removed)**
approx. 300ml vegetable oil
200g potato starch
2 teaspoons salt
½ teaspoon ground white pepper
2 teaspoons caster sugar
2 teaspoons ground ginger
**½ teaspoon Chinese five spice
powder**
2 red chillies, diced, to garnish
**Sweet Chilli Sauce (see page 156),
to serve**

1 Separate the squid tentacles so that you have bunches of 3 or 4 tentacles joined together. Cut open the squid body by making a vertical cut through one side of it. Open up the body, lay it flat, and make shallow diagonal cuts across the inside of the body in a criss-cross or diamond pattern. Cut the body into small, even-sized, rectangles, approx. 5 x 2.5cm.

2 Fill a wok with vegetable oil so that it is at least 7.5cm deep. Heat to 180°C over a medium heat (to test the temperature, see page 149).

3 While you're waiting for the oil to heat up, put the potato starch in a shallow bowl. In a separate bowl, mix the salt, white pepper, sugar, ground ginger and five spice powder together, then set it aside for later.

4 Working with one or two pieces of squid at a time, coat the squid in the potato starch and gently shake off the excess. Place the coated pieces of squid on a plate in a single layer until you're ready to deep-fry them, separating the tentacles from the body pieces as they both require different cooking times.

5 When the oil is hot enough, carefully lower one-third of the squid into the hot oil. (You need to cook it in batches to avoid overcrowding the pan.) As you drop the squid into the hot oil the pieces will curl up. Keep turning them until they are golden brown and crisp all over – the tentacles will take 2–3 minutes and the body parts will take 3–4 minutes. Remove the first batch of crispy fried squid from the pan using a Chinese wire strainer or slotted spoon and transfer to a plate lined with kitchen paper to absorb some of the excess fat.

6 Immediately sprinkle a pinch of the salt-and-pepper mixture over the deep-fried squid and set aside while you cook the rest. Make sure you bring the temperature of the oil back up to 180°C between batches. To serve, scatter over the diced red chillies and accompany with Sweet Chilli Sauce.

 LISA'S TIP The best way to know when the squid is ready is when tubes and the tentacles start to curl up. Don't let it become too curled otherwise it will be overcooked.

Crispy Quinoa & Scallop Balls

香酥藜麥帶子球

This dish is made with quinoa, a gluten-free grain that is high in protein. Our grandmother used to tell us that although it originates from Peru, the fact that it was pronounced 'Kin wah' – which is a Chinese name – meant it must have been popular in China too. The grain is a good source of dietary fibre and phosphorus and is high in magnesium and iron. It is a source of calcium, and thus is useful for vegans and those who are lactose intolerant. Quinoa goes really well with scallops because its earthy flavours contrast well with the salty sea flavour of the scallops.

MAKES **10 balls**

PREPARATION TIME **30 minutes, plus 1 hour chilling time**

COOKING TIME **10 minutes**

150g quinoa

300ml chicken stock (or water)

1 bay leaf

1 onion

2 garlic cloves

2 tablespoons vegetable oil

4 rashers of bacon, finely diced

1 tablespoon chilli bean paste

100g grated Parmesan cheese

300g scallops, cut into 2cm dice

2 tablespoons chopped parsley

350g breadcrumbs

4 eggs

2 teaspoons salt, plus a pinch

1 teaspoon caster sugar, plus a pinch

½ teaspoon white pepper

300ml vegetable oil, for deep-frying

Sweet Chilli Sauce (see page 156),
  to serve

1 Put the quinoa, chicken stock (or water) and bay leaf in a medium saucepan and bring to the boil over a high heat. Cook for 20–25 minutes until all of the stock has been absorbed. Remove the pan from the heat and discard the bay leaf. Meanwhile, place the onion and garlic in a food processor and blitz to a smooth paste.

2 Heat a wok over a high heat with the vegetable oil. Scrape in the onion and garlic mixture and add the bacon and chilli bean paste. Stir-fry for 7–8 minutes until the onions are golden and the bacon is crisp.

3 Meanwhile, tip the cooked quinoa into a mixing bowl. Add the cooked bacon and onion along with the Parmesan, scallops, parsley and 100g of the breadcrumbs.

4 Break an egg into the mixture and stir well until all the ingredients are combined. Season with 2 teaspoons of the salt, 1 teaspoon of the sugar and the white pepper and mix again. Cover the bowl with clingfilm and transfer the mixture to the fridge to firm up for 1 hour.

5 Meanwhile, break the remaining eggs into a shallow bowl, season with the pinch of salt and pinch of sugar and beat well together. Place the remaining breadcrumbs in a separate shallow bowl or dish.

6 Remove the quinoa mixture from the fridge and shape it into 10 small balls in the palms of your hands. Dip each ball first into the beaten eggs, then into the breadcrumbs, coating it well on all sides. Set aside on a plate.

7 Preheat the vegetable oil to 180°C in a wok over a high heat (to test the temperature, see page 149). Carefully lower 4–5 quinoa balls into the hot oil and cook for 4–5 minutes until golden brown. Remove the crispy balls from the hot oil using a slotted spoon and drain on kitchen paper while you cook the rest. Serve warm with Sweet Chilli Sauce.

 LISA'S TIP Fresh scallops can be expensive, so an alternative is to buy frozen scallops from a Chinese cash-and-carry. Just defrost a portion and dice up into the mixture.

Crab Dumplings
蟹黃燒賣

I still remember the sharp pain I felt when I got bitten by a crab in the fish market, aged 6, and how Dad nobly took that particular crab back home and cooked it up in revenge. Suffice to say I learnt my lesson and I have never touched another live crab pincer since! Crab has a very delicate flavour, which is enhanced here by the addition of king prawns to give the dumplings a bit of texture. Fresh coriander lifts the flavours and binds the ingredients together.

MAKES **12**
PREPARATION TIME **20 minutes, plus
20 minutes resting time**
COOKING TIME **10 minutes**

**150g raw, peeled king prawns,
 deveined**
100g white crab meat
50g finely chopped coriander
**1cm piece of fresh root ginger,
 finely chopped**
1 teaspoon very finely chopped chilli
1 teaspoon salt
1 teaspoon caster sugar
½ teaspoon white pepper
½ teaspoon sesame oil
1 tablespoon potato starch
1 tablespoon water
For the dumpling wrappers
120g wheat starch
70g tapioca flour
1 teaspoon salt
2 teaspoons vegetable oil
180–200ml boiling water
**Sweet Chilli Sauce (see page 156),
 to serve**

1 Rinse the king prawns under cold running water and pat dry on kitchen paper. Slice each king prawn into 4 pieces, and then flatten each piece with a large knife or hammer until it is 5mm thick. Transfer the prawns to a bowl.
2 Drain off any water from the crab meat and combine the crab with the prawns. Add the coriander, ginger, chilli, salt, sugar, pepper, sesame oil, potato starch and water. Mix the ingredients in a clockwise direction until they come together in a sticky paste. Cover the bowl with clingfilm and set aside in the fridge for 15 minutes while you prepare the pastry.
3 To make the dumpling wrappers, put the wheat starch and tapioca flour in a medium bowl and add the salt and oil. Mix the ingredients together with a wooden spoon, and then quickly add the boiling water and mix fast until the dough comes together in a ball. Use your hand to knead the dough until smooth. Cover the bowl with a damp cloth and set aside to rest at room temperature for 20 minutes.
4 Turn out the dough onto a floured work surface, knead and roll into a log, approx. 18cm long. Cut into 12 even pieces. Flatten each piece with the palm of the hand, and then roll out to a circle approx. 6cm in diameter using a rolling pin.
5 To assemble the dumplings, place 1 heaped tablespoon of the filling in the centre of each pastry. Scoop the pastry into the centre so that it holds all the filling and twist the edge to seal the dumpling. The shape will resemble a round ball with a flowered edge like a translucent money-bag. Arrange the finished dumplings spaced 1cm apart inside a bamboo steamer lined with baking parchment.
6 To cook the dumplings, fill a wok with water so that it is just over one-quarter full. Set a round cake rack in the centre, cover with a lid and bring to the boil over a high heat.
7 Place the bamboo steamer inside the wok and steam the dumplings for 10 minutes. Remove from the heat and leave the lid of the steamer slightly ajar to allow some steam to escape for 2 minutes. Serve hot with Sweet Chilli Sauce.

Crab Claws

蟹鉗

Crab claws are a symbolic dim sum dish that is traditionally enjoyed at Chinese weddings. It's a favourite on the wedding menu because it represents joy, celebration and completeness. It is essentially a crab claw encased in a prawn mousse and breadcrumbs then deep-fried. The crab claw is the sweetest nugget of the crab and the easiest to eat. It is always a huge honour to host a wedding at Sweet Mandarin. The ceremony is usually opened with firecrackers, but once they have finished and everyone has returned to their seats the food begins to flow.

MAKES **12 claws**
PREPARATION TIME **20 minutes, plus
40 minutes chilling time**
COOKING TIME **20 minutes**

**12 cooked crab claws (thawed on
    kitchen paper if frozen to absorb
    the excess moisture)**
200g plain flour
250g panko breadcrumbs
1 large egg
vegetable oil, for deep-frying
**Sweet Chilli Sauce (see page 156),
    to serve**
For the king prawn paste
**300g raw, peeled king prawns,
    deveined**
1 spring onion, finely sliced
2cm piece of fresh root ginger
1 shallot, finely diced
1 garlic clove, crushed
1 teaspoon white sugar
1 teaspoon salt
1 tablespoon potato starch
1 teaspoon sesame oil
1 teaspoon Shaoxing rice wine
**3 teaspoons vegetable oil, plus extra
    for greasing**

1 Combine all the ingredients for the king prawn paste in a food processor and blitz to a smooth paste. Scoop out into a bowl, cover with clingfilm and transfer to the fridge to firm up for 20 minutes.

2 Dry the crab claws really well on kitchen paper – this is important or the king prawn paste won't stick to them.

3 Tip the flour onto one plate and the panko breadcrumbs into a deep container. Beat the egg in a little bowl ready for coating the crab claws later.

4 Remove the king prawn paste from the fridge and grease your hands with a little oil. Shape the king prawn mixture into 12 balls, approx. 4cm in diameter. Insert a claw into each prawn ball and mould the paste around the shell to form an even coating. Dip the coated claws first in the flour, then in the beaten egg and finally in the panko breadcrumbs and arrange on a plate. Transfer to the fridge for 20 minutes to set.

5 Fill a wok half full with vegetable oil and preheat to 180°C over a high heat (to test the temperature, see page 149). Lower the crab claws one at a time into the hot oil and cook for 4-5 minutes, turning frequently until golden brown. Cook in batches of 4 to prevent overcrowding the pan. Use a Chinese wire net or a slotted spoon to scoop out the crab claws and drain on kitchen paper. Serve with Sweet Chilli Sauce.

LISA'S TIP To ensure the crab claws are coated evenly, place the panko breadcrumbs in a deep container. Once one side is coated turn it over so that it's immersed in the panko breadcrumbs.

Lobster Dumplings

龍蝦餃

When I first tasted black truffle I was overwhelmed by its delicious and powerful flavour, a taste I had never come across before. It had a spirit of wanderlust, as if I had stuck my tongue in a bed of intense greens buried deep in the earth. I love learning about new foods and never grow tired of fusing ingredients from different cuisines, so when I got back to Sweet Mandarin I started experimenting with this new flavour. I discovered that truffle goes wonderfully with king prawns and lobster, hence the invention of this dish, which makes a wonderful, indulgent treat for a special occasion.

MAKES **12**
PREPARATION TIME **50 minutes, plus
15 minutes chilling time**
COOKING TIME **10 minutes**

700g live lobster
2 spring onions
**200g raw, peeled king prawns,
  deveined**
**3 x 2cm pieces of fresh root ginger,
  finely chopped**
**200g chestnut mushrooms, finely
  chopped**
3 celery sticks, finely chopped
1 teaspoon salt
pinch of white pepper
1 teaspoon caster sugar
1 tablespoon light soy sauce
1 tablespoon sesame oil
1 tablespoon Shaoxing rice wine
2 tablespoons water
1 tablespoon potato starch
12 wonton wrappers
**1 black truffle, shaved into
  12 shavings**
vegetable oil, for greasing
**Sweet Chilli Sauce (see page 156),
  to serve**

1 Bring a large pot of salted water to the boil. Plunge the lobster into the water head first and partially cook until it turns bright red, approx. 2 minutes. Drain the lobster and cool under cold running water. Twist off the tail and the claws, and use a hammer to crack them open. Remove the meat from inside the tail and claws and chop into 1cm pieces.

2 Cut the spring onions into quarters lengthways, and then into small pieces. Set aside. Cut each king prawn into 4 pieces, and then flatten each piece with a large knife or hammer until it is 5mm thick. Transfer to a mixing bowl.

3 Add the lobster, ginger, mushrooms, celery, spring onions, salt, pepper, sugar, light soy sauce, sesame oil, Shaoxing wine, water and potato starch. Mix the ingredients in a clockwise direction until they come together in a sticky paste. Cover the bowl with clingfilm and set aside in the fridge for 15 minutes while you prepare the wrappers.

4 To assemble the dumplings, trim the corners off the wonton wrappers (with a knife or scissors) to make the pastry round instead of square. This dumpling will be similar in shape to a Siu Mai (see page 14). To assemble the dumplings, cup the fingers on your left hand and place a wonton wrapper inside your cupped hand. Place 1 heaped tablespoon of the filling in the centre of the wrapper. Gather up the sides of the pastry around the filling and squeeze them together to form a little open-topped square parcel. Holding the dumpling between your thumb and index finger, carefully smooth the surface of the filling with a teaspoon or knife so that it is nice and level, and then place a shaving of truffle in the centre. Arrange the filled dumpling on a lightly oiled plate and set aside while you assemble the rest.

5 To cook the dumplings, fill a wok with water so that it is just over one-quarter full. Set a round cake rack in the centre, cover with a lid and bring to the boil over a high heat. Place the bamboo steamer inside the wok and steam the dumplings for 8–10 minutes. Serve with Sweet Chilli Sauce.

 LISA'S TIP Black truffle is very indulgent, so when making this dim sum you need only a small amount to enhance the filling's flavours or you can substitute it with a few drops of truffle oil.

Vegetables

蔬菜

Porcini Dumplings

牛肝菌餃

Porcini mushrooms can be found in Europe, Asia and North America. The Italian name porcino translates as 'piglet', and echoes the term *suilli*, literally 'hog mushrooms', used by the Ancient Romans. Porcini mushrooms are well suited to drying, which intensifies their flavour. I think they work really well in this dim sum.

MAKES **12**

PREPARATION TIME **30 minutes, plus 15 minutes soaking and 35 minutes resting time**

COOKING TIME **10 minutes**

20 dried Chinese mushrooms

40g dried porcini mushrooms

1 tablespoon vegetable oil

4 garlic cloves, crushed

25g chives, finely chopped

200g chestnut mushrooms, diced

200g cooked chestnuts, cut into
   3mm dice

50ml water

1 teaspoon salt

2 teaspoons caster sugar

2 teaspoons oyster sauce

1 teaspoon Shaoxing rice wine

½ teaspoon sesame oil

1 teaspoon potato starch

For the dumpling wrappers

120g wheat starch

70g tapioca flour

1 teaspoon salt

2 teaspoons vegetable oil

180–200ml boiling water

sriracha hot sauce and light soy
   sauce, to serve

1 Place all the dried mushrooms in a bowl, cover with hot water and set aside to soak for 15 minutes. Drain well, discarding the soaking liquor. Cut into small pieces.

2 To make the filling, heat a wok over a medium heat and add the oil. Fry the garlic and chives for 2–3 minutes until soft but not coloured. Add the mushrooms and chestnuts and stir-fry for 5 minutes until the chestnuts are slightly browned. Add the water, salt, sugar, oyster sauce, Shaoxing wine, sesame oil and potato starch and cook for 5 minutes, stirring. Remove from the heat, transfer to a bowl and cover with clingfilm, then set aside to cool in the fridge for 15 minutes.

3 Meanwhile, make the dumpling wrappers. Put the wheat starch and tapioca flour in a medium bowl and add the salt and oil. Mix together in a clockwise direction with a wooden spoon, then gradually add enough boiling water so that the dough comes together in a ball. It will be bright white in colour, like snow. Use your hand to knead the dough until smooth. Cover the bowl with a damp cloth and set aside to rest at room temperature for 20 minutes.

4 Turn out the dough onto a floured work surface, knead and roll into a log, approx. 18cm long. Cut into 12 even pieces. Flatten each piece with the palm of your hand, and then roll out to a circle approx. 6cm in diameter using a rolling pin.

5 To assemble the dumplings, place 1 heaped tablespoon of the filling in the centre of each wrapper, wet the edges with your finger and fold in the 3 sides of the dumpling so that they meet in the middle. Squeeze the edges together to form a pyramind and use you thumb and index finger to crimp the tip. Place the dumplings 1cm apart on parchment paper in a bamboo steamer.

6 Fill a wok with water so that it is just over one-quarter full. Set a round cake rack in the centre, cover with a lid and bring to the boil over a high heat. Place the bamboo steamer inside the wok and steam for 10 minutes. Remove from the heat and leave the lid of the steamer slightly ajar to allow some steam to escape for 2 minutes. Serve with sriracha hot sauce and light soy sauce.

 LISA'S TIP You can replace the chestnuts with water chestnuts, if you wish.

Pumpkin Dumplings
南瓜餃

This recipe came about during an experiment in the Sweet Mandarin Cookery School on a team-building day. On this occasion, we had given the students pumpkin and pine nuts and asked them to come up with a dish in 30 minutes. You might think this is a strange combination of ingredients, but they complement each other really well. The sweetness and soft pulp of the pumpkin works perfectly with the rich creamy flavour of the pine nuts and the crunchy texture adds an extra dimension. Pine nuts are a great source of omega-3 fats, an important nutrient not only for a healthy heart but also for boosting the brain. They are also very rich in vitamin E and zinc, two antioxidants that can help with important functions in the body like the immune system and fertility.

MAKES **12**
PREPARATION TIME **25 minutes, plus
20 minutes resting time**
COOKING TIME **10 minutes**

**300g pumpkin or squash flesh, cut
into 2mm cubes**
**100g tinned chickpeas, drained
and rinsed**
2 tablespoons vegetable oil
1 garlic clove, crushed
**1cm piece of fresh root ginger,
finely chopped**
1 teaspoon paprika
½ teaspoon dried sage
1 tablespoon light soy sauce
1 tablespoon Shaoxing rice wine
1 teaspoon sesame oil
1 teaspoon salt
1 teaspoon caster sugar
1 tablespoon potato starch
50g toasted pine nuts
**Sweet Chilli Sauce (see page 156),
to serve**
For the dumpling skins
110ml boiling water
½ teaspoon salt
**200g strong white flour, plus extra
for dusting**

1 First make the dumpling skins. Measure out the boiling water into a jug and stir in the salt to dissolve it. Sift the flour 2–3 times into a mixing bowl. Pour in the salty water and mix to a stiff paste. Knead in the bowl for 10 minutes until smooth. Cover the bowl with clingfilm and set aside to rest at room temperature for 20 minutes.
2 Turn out the dough onto a floured surface and divide it into 12 even pieces. Roll out each piece to form 12 x 10cm circles using a rolling pin. Cover the dumpling skins with a damp tea towel and set aside to rest while you make the filling.
3 To make the filling, combine the pumpkin or squash and chickpeas in a medium saucepan. Cover with cold water and cook over a high heat for 10 minutes until soft. Drain and set aside.
4 Heat 1 tablespoon of the oil in a wok over a high heat, add the garlic and ginger and stir-fry for 2–3 minutes until fragrant. Add the softened pumpkin and chickpeas, and season with paprika, sage, light soy sauce, Shaoxing wine, sesame oil, salt, sugar and potato starch. Stir well until thoroughly combined.
5 Transfer the filling to a bowl and mash with a potato masher until it forms a thick paste. Stir in the toasted pine nuts and mix well. Leave to cool for 20 minutes.
6 To assemble the dumplings, wet your index finger with water and moisten the outer rim of each dumpling wrapper. Place 1 heaped tablespoon of the filling in the centre of each wrapper and bring the edges to the centre, then mould them together to seal the dumpling. It should resemble a small ball. Using the palm of your hand, flatten the ball so that it's like a small patty.
7 To cook the dumplings, heat a medium frying pan over a medium heat and add 1 tablespoon of oil. Put in the dumplings and pan-fry for 1–2 minutes, without turning, until the base of each one forms a slightly golden brown crust. Pour in 70ml water, cover the pan with a lid and continue to cook until most of the water has evaporated, approx. 5–6 minutes. Cook for a further 2–3 minutes until the pastry has firmed up. Serve with Sweet Chilli Sauce.

 LISA'S TIP When making the dumplings into round patty shapes, put them on a floured surface and use your hands to mould them.

Pyramid Mushroom & Carrot Dumplings

蒸蘑菇粽

Our entire family wears glasses and our mother still shakes her head and says we are wasted – one of us should have been an optician and we would have saved a tonne of money! She did try though, bless her, to make dishes using carrots including this dim sum. Carrots would help us see better and even help us see in the dark! Our brother hearing that carrots gave super powers in the form of night vision ate as many as he could one dinner until our father piped up that he was turning a visibly bright shade of orange. Our brother stopped midway through his final carrot and ran to the bathroom to inspect whether he had indeed gone a shade of orange. We still chuckle when we make this dim sum and eat them together.

MAKES **12**

PREPARATION TIME **45 minutes plus 30 minutes resting time**

COOKING TIME **10 minutes**

300g skinless chicken breast fillets

1 tablespoon vegetable oil

100g straw mushrooms, diced

100g shiitake mushrooms, soaked and diced

100g button mushrooms, diced

2 carrots, peeled and diced

2 garlic cloves, crushed

5mm piece of fresh root ginger, finely chopped

1 teaspoon salt

1 teaspoon caster sugar

¼ teaspoon white pepper

½ teaspoon sesame oil

1 teaspoon oyster sauce

1 tablespoon potato starch

1 teaspoon light soy sauce

2 spring onions, diced

For the dumping wrappers

120g wheat starch, plus extra for dusting

70g tapioca flour

1 teaspoon salt

2 teaspoons vegetable oil

180–200ml boiling water

1 First make the filling. Put the chicken in a food processor and blitz until it forms a thick paste.

2 Add the oil to a wok over a high heat and stir-fry all three types of mushroom, the carrots, garlic, ginger, salt, sugar and pepper for 2–3 minutes. Then remove from the heat and drain the mixture in a colander and leave to cool. Once cooled, transfer the mixture into a bowl and add the chicken, sesame oil, oyster sauce, potato starch, light soy sauce and diced spring onions. Mix with a wooden spoon in a clockwise direction for 3 minutes until thoroughly combined. Cover with clingfilm and transfer to the fridge to rest for 10 minutes.

3 To make the dumpling wrappers, put the wheat starch and tapioca flour in a medium bowl and add the salt and oil. Mix together in a clockwise direction with a wooden spoon, and then gradually add enough boiling water so that the dough comes together in a ball. It will be bright white in colour, like snow. Use your hand to knead the dough until smooth. Cover the bowl with a damp cloth and set aside to rest at room temperature for 20 minutes.

4 Turn out the dough onto a floured work surface, knead and then roll into a log, approx. 18cm long. Cut into 12 even pieces. Flatten each piece with the palm of your hand, and then roll out to a circle approx. 6cm in diameter using a rolling pin.

5 To assemble the dumplings, place 1 heaped tablespoon of the filling in the centre of each square of pastry and dampen around the edges with a little water. This dumpling will be shaped like a pyramid. To create this shape, fold in the 3 sides so that they meet in the middle, and then squeeze the sides and edges together to form a little pyramid shape (see page 103). Use your thumb and index finger to crimp the tip. Arrange the finished dumplings in a bamboo steamer lined with baking parchment.

6 To cook the dumplings, fill a saucepan or wok just over one quarter full with water and place a cake rack in the centre. Cover the wok with a lid and bring to the boil over a high heat. Place the bamboo steamer inside the wok and steam the dumplings for 10 minutes. Serve hot.

Money-bags with Beans, Sweetcorn & Red Pepper

金錢包

This dim sum looks a million dollars and is also good for your well-being. When we used to go to the Chinese supermarket with our grandmother, she always used to tell us to pick the dark red peppers, not the light red ones, as they contained more vitamins and goodness. She was absolutely right: peppers are crammed with vitamin B6, which helps reduce heart disease and stroke, as well as vitamins C and E, which are antioxidants.

MAKES 12
PREPARATION TIME 20 minutes
COOKING TIME 15 minutes

150g tinned kidney beans, drained and rinsed

150g tinned chickpeas, drained and rinsed

2cm piece of fresh root ginger, finely chopped

150g red peppers, deseeded and finely diced

150g avocado, finely diced

150g tinned sweetcorn (drained weight)

1 tablespoon hoisin sauce

1 teaspoon salt

1 teaspoon caster sugar

1 teaspoon white pepper

1 tablespoon light soy sauce

1 teaspoon sesame oil

1 tablespoon potato starch

12 wonton wrappers (made for deep-frying)

200ml vegetable oil

salad cream, to serve

1 Put the kidney beans and chickpeas in a medium saucepan, cover with plenty of cold water and bring to the boil over a high heat. Boil for 15 minutes until soft. Drain well.

2 Transfer the beans and chickpeas to a food processor, add the ginger and blitz to a chunky purée. Scoop the mixture into a bowl and add the red peppers, avocado and sweetcorn. Season with hoisin sauce, salt, sugar, pepper, light soy sauce, sesame oil and potato starch. Mix in a clockwise direction until the ingredients are fully incorporated.

3 To assemble the dumplings, peel off one of the wonton wrappers and place it in the palm of your hand. Scoop 1 heaped tablespoon of the filling into the centre and draw up the sides to enclose the filling. To close the wrapper, twist the ends together at the top to form a money-bag shape. Repeat with the rest of the wrappers and filling to form 12 parcels altogether.

4 To cook the parcels, heat the oil to 180°C in a wok over a high heat (to test the temperature, see page 149). Carefully lower the money-bags into the hot oil and cook for 5–6 minutes, flipping them over until both sides are golden brown. Serve with salad cream for dipping.

 LISA'S TIP The wonton wrappers have potato starch to separate each sheet. To ensure the wonton wrapper is fully closed, dab some water around the edges so that it will stick together when twisting the edges.

Crispy Siu Mai

脆香燒賣

Asparagus is one of those vegetables that my mother would serve when it was our birthday as she said it was very expensive. Each person had their ration of two stalks of asparagus and that was our luxury for the year. I ate my two stalks very slowly – so slowly that my grandmother questioned whether I didn't like it and whether I wanted to give her my portion, to which I shook my head and ate a bit quicker. Asparagus is not only delicious when cooked al dente, so that it still has a bite, but it is also filled with vitamin E, which helps keep the heart and the immune system strong to ward off illness. The asparagus in this dim sum lifts the softer filling of the chickpea and sweet potato. Don't overcook the asparagus, as its best eaten with a crunch to it.

MAKES **12**

PREPARATION TIME **20 minutes, plus 5 minutes chilling**

COOKING TIME **15 minutes**

100g asparagus

180g sweet potatoes

50g chickpeas

1 spring onion, diced

2–3 x 2cm pieces of fresh root ginger

1 teaspoon salt

pinch of white pepper

1 teaspoon white sugar

1 tablespoon light soy sauce

1 teaspoon sesame oil

1 tablespoon Shaoxing rice wine

1 tablespoon water

2 teaspoons potato starch

12 wonton wrappers

12 peas

300ml vegetable oil, for deep-frying

Sweet Chilli Sauce (see page 156), to serve

1 Boil the asparagus for 5 minutes then set aside. Boil the sweet potatoes and chickpeas in a medium saucepan over a high heat for 15 minutes. Remove from the heat and drain.

2 Transfer the asparagus, sweet potato and chickpeas to a blender and blitz together until they form a thick paste. Add the spring onion and mix together. Add the ginger, salt, pepper, sugar, light soy sauce, sesame oil, Shaoxing wine, water and potato starch. Mix in a clockwise direction for 1 minute until thoroughly combined. Transfer the filling to the fridge to chill for 5 minutes.

3 Trim the corners of the wonton wrappers so that the wrappers are round in shape. Cup the fingers on your left hand and place a wrapper on the fingers. Put 1 tablespoon of filling in the centre of the wrapper. Then, using your fingers, squeeze the filling into the pastry so that it becomes a little square. Place the dumpling in between your thumb and index finger and, using a spoon or knife, flatten the filling that protrudes up when shaping the main body of the dumpling. This will shape the dumpling so that it can stand upright. Decorate the dumpling with a pea in the centre.

4 To cook the dumplings, heat a wok with the oil over a high heat (to test the temperature, see page 149). Carefully drop the dumplings in the hot oil and cook for 5–7 minutes. (Cook in batches if necessary.) Serve with Sweet Chilli Sauce.

Sweet Potato, Prawn & Pinto Bean Fritters

芸豆蕃薯餅

Whenever I cook sweet potatoes it reminds me of the time in Beijing when I was chased down the street by a street vendor shaking a hot potato at me because I wasn't prepared to pay an outrageous price like ten pounds for it. Luckily I was saved when a stationary bicycle fell across his path, but it didn't prevent him from lobbing the potato at me – missing my head by inches. The experience certainly taught me a lesson: bartering is a way of life in China and you should never ask the price unless you are prepared to buy. This is one of my favourite dim sum – not only are the dumplings easy to make and delicious but sweet potato is high in beta-carotene, which helps the eyes, as well as vitamin E to improve the skin. Sweet potato is also very filling – so if you are dieting, this dim sum should help keep hunger pangs at bay.

MAKES **6**
PREPARATION TIME **30 minutes, plus overnight soaking**
COOKING TIME **10 minutes**

100g dried pinto beans
vegetable oil, for greasing
2 medium sweet potatoes, peeled and
    cut into 5cm chunks
2cm piece of fresh root ginger, grated
1 garlic clove, crushed
½ spring onion, finely sliced
1 shallot, finely diced
400g raw, peeled king prawns,
    deveined
1 egg
½ teaspoon salt
1 teaspoon caster sugar
¼ teaspoon white pepper
1 teaspoon sesame oil
2 tablespoon potato starch
Sweet Chilli Sauce (see page 156),
    to serve

1 Place the pinto beans in a pan, cover with cold water and set aside to soak overnight. Drain, discarding the soaking liquor.
2 Preheat the oven to 180°C/gas 4 and grease a baking tray with vegetable oil.
3 Place the soaked pinto beans in a medium saucepan with the sweet potatoes. Cover with fresh water and bring to the boil over a high heat. Cook for 15 minutes until soft. Drain well. Transfer the cooked sweet potato and beans to a large bowl and mash with a potato masher until smooth. Stir in the ginger, garlic, spring onion and shallot and mix well.
4 Wash the king prawns under cold running water and pat dry on kitchen paper. Chop each prawn into 4 pieces, and then flatten each piece using a large knife or hammer until it is 5mm thick. Add the prawns to the bowl with the sweet potato and beans.
5 Crack in the egg and season the mixture with salt, sugar, pepper and sesame oil. Add the potato starch and mix the filling in a clockwise direction until all the ingredients come together in a sticky paste.
6 To shape the dumplings, divide the mixture into 6 even portions and shape into 5cm balls in the palms of your hands – it helps if you grease your hands first with a little vegetable oil. Transfer the patties to the baking tray and bake for 10 minutes, turning halfway through cooking. Serve with Sweet Chilli Sauce.

 LISA'S TIP To add more texture you can grate the raw sweet potato and add it to the filling mixture. This can be then cooked from raw.

Spring Onion Pancakes

醬香蔥餅

These spring roll pancakes are traditionally enjoyed as a delicacy for breakfast. This version is made with XO sauce to give the pancakes a bit of a kick. XO is an acronym, which stands for extra old cognac – even though there isn't any cognac in it. When I asked my father why would a sauce be named after XO cognac but not have any cognac in it, his response was one word: 'status'. Indeed, XO sauce is expensive and was introduced to Hong Kong in the 1980s to the upper echelons of society who enjoyed cognac. *Vogue* China once called it the 'caviar of the East' and if there is one thing that you should try it's this spicy, dried scallop sauce packed with umami flavours. XO sauce certainly makes these spring onion pancakes extra indulgent and delicious.

MAKES **10**
PREPARATION TIME **30 minutes**
COOKING TIME **5–10 minutes**

220g plain flour, plus extra
    for dusting
1 teaspoon salt
150ml warm water
3 tablespoons vegetable oil, or more
    as needed
6 spring onions, finely sliced
4 tablespoons XO sauce (available
    from Chinese supermarkets)

1 Sift the flour and salt into a bowl. Pour in the water a little at a time and mix to a stiff dough. Turn out the dough onto a floured surface and divide into 2 even pieces. Roll out each piece into a flat rectangle approx. 20cm long and 2cm thick. Brush each rectangle with 1 tablespoon of the oil, then scatter over the spring onions and spread with the XO sauce.

2 Roll up the rectangles, starting at the shortest edge, to form 2 Swiss roll shapes, then cut each Swiss roll into 4 even pieces. Flatten each piece with the palm of your hand, then roll it into a round pancake, approx. 10 cm in diameter, using a rolling pin.

3 Heat a wok over a high heat with the remaining 1 tablespoon of the oil. Fry the pancakes for 4–5 minutes on each side until golden brown – you may need to do this in batches. Transfer to a serving plate and cover with foil to keep warm while you cook the rest, adding more oil to the pan as necessary. Serve warm.

Tofu & Chinese Mushroom Quenelles

冬菇豆腐丸

I love watching *Masterchef* and one of the ways of presenting a dish that has always been on my mind is the quenelle. This is my version of a quenelle with Chinese ingredients and flavours. The ingredients came to me when I reached into my satchel and pulled out a bag of dried Chinese mushrooms – we had had a case of them delivered to Sweet Mandarin and I had taken a bag back with me to enjoy at home. They looked like they were artificial – all the water had been sucked out of them and they snapped apart like a cracker. The aroma when I opened the packet was intensely sweet, woody and slightly intoxicating. This combination is definitely a match made in food heaven. The Chinese mushrooms contrast well with tofu, which is flavourless and almost begging to be infused with this umami flavour.

MAKES **10**
PREPARATION TIME **20 minutes, plus
15 minutes soaking and 20 minutes
chilling time**
COOKING TIME **25 minutes**

12 dried Chinese mushrooms
**approx. 250g fresh firm tofu
   (6 square blocks)**
1 medium onion, finely diced
2 spring onions, finely sliced
1 teaspoon salt, plus a pinch
1 teaspoon caster sugar, plus a pinch
1 teaspoon light soy sauce
1 egg
2 tablespoons potato starch
**150ml vegetable oil for deep-frying,
   plus 1 tablespoon**
100ml chicken stock
1 teaspoon oyster sauce
drop of sesame oil
drop of Shaoxing rice wine

1 Place the mushrooms in a bowl, cover with hot water and set aside to soak for 15 minutes. Drain well, discarding the soaking liquor, and cut into fine dice. Place the tofu in a bowl and mash well with a large tablespoon until it breaks up into small pieces.
2 Reserve 1 tablespoon of the diced mushrooms, onion and spring onions for the sauce and add the rest to the bowl with the tofu. Season the tofu mixture with 1 teaspoon of the salt, 1 teaspoon of the sugar and the light soy sauce and crack in the egg. Finally add 1 tablespoon of the potato starch. Stir the mixture in a clockwise direction until the ingredients come together in a sticky paste.
3 To shape the tofu balls, remove tablespoons of the mixture at a time and shape into 10 ovals using 2 tablespoons to achieve a quenelle shape. Transfer the tofu quenelles to a plate, cover with clingfilm and set aside in the fridge to firm up for 20 minutes.
4 To cook the tofu balls, heat 150ml vegetable oil to 180°C over a high heat (to test the temperature, see page 149). Carefully lower the tofu quenelle into the hot oil and cook for 5–7 minutes until golden all over, turning with a slotted spoon to prevent them from sticking together. Remove the quenelles with a Chinese net or slotted spoon and set aside on kitchen paper to drain. Drain and clean the wok.
5 To make the sauce, set the clean wok over a high heat and add the 1 tablespoon of vegetable oil. Put in the reserved mushrooms, onion and spring onion and stir-fry for 3–4 minutes. Pour in the chicken stock, bring to the boil and season with the pinch of salt and sugar, the oyster sauce, sesame oil and Shaoxing wine. Mix the remaining 1 tablespoon of potato starch with 2 tablespoons of cold water in a little bowl and pour into the wok to thicken the sauce. To serve, arrange the fried quenelles on a serving plate and pour over the sauce.

 LISA'S TIP To garnish this dish, place blanched broccoli florets around the plate. Place the fried tofu quenelles in the centre and spoon the sauce over them.

Salt & Pepper Tofu
椒鹽豆腐

If you are vegetarian or wanting to follow a vegetarian diet, I cannot recommend this dim sum enough. Tofu, also called bean curd, is a food made by coagulating soya juice and then pressing the resulting curds into soft white blocks. It is a component in many East Asian and South-east Asian cuisines. There are many different varieties of tofu, including fresh tofu and tofu that has been processed in some way. Tofu has a subtle flavour and can be used in savoury and sweet dishes. It is low in calories, contains relatively large amounts of protein and little fat. It is high in iron and, depending on the coagulant used in manufacturing, may also be high in calcium and/or magnesium. Tofu in its natural form is soft but when fried, as in this recipe, it turns crispy. This crispy texture works wonderfully with the salt and pepper mix.

SERVES **2**
PREPARATION TIME **15 minutes**
COOKING TIME **15 minutes**

2 x 100g blocks of firm tofu
1 teaspoon salt
½ teaspoon black pepper
4 tablespoons potato starch
4 tablespoons vegetable oil
1 green pepper, deseeded and
   finely diced
1 small onion, finely diced
2 garlic cloves, finely chopped
1 red chilli, finely diced
1 teaspoon Shaoxing rice wine
For the dry spice mix
½ teaspoon ground ginger
½ teaspoon Chinese five spice
   powder
2 teaspoons caster sugar
½ teaspoon salt

1 Drain the tofu, pat dry on kitchen paper and chop into 2.5cm cubes. Place the pieces of tofu in a bowl, season well with salt and pepper and sprinkle over the potato starch. Mix well with your hands to coat the tofu on all sides.

2 Combine the dry spice ingredients in a separate bowl and mix well together.

3 To cook the tofu, heat a wok over a high heat and add 3 tablespoons of the oil. Once the oil is nice and hot, add the tofu and fry for 4–5 minutes until golden brown on all sides. Remove the tofu from the pan with a slotted spoon and set aside on kitchen paper to absorb the excess oil.

4 Heat a clean wok over a high heat and add the remaining 1 tablespoon of vegetable oil. Put in the pepper, onion, garlic and chilli and stir-fry for 2 minutes. Add the fried tofu cubes and cook for a further 3–4 minutes, stirring. Sprinkle over the dry spice mix and toss together. Finally drizzle over the Shaoxing wine and toss well for 1 minute. Serve immediately.

 LISA'S TIP Be careful when deep-frying the tofu cubes as the tofu has a high water content. Use a slotted spoon to drop the tofu cubes into the oil and place on kitchen paper to drain when cooked.

Classic Turnip Cake

蘿蔔糕

In Hong Kong, Chinese New Year is celebrated like Christmas is in the West – with families gathering and eating together. One of the symbolic breakfast dishes is Chinese radish cake – although it's not really like cake at all, it's more like a stodgy pudding, but delicious nonetheless. If made well, this dish will pacify the most critical backseat chef for life. I learnt to make it the hard way and my first attempt was disastrous – if you had thrown it up on the ceiling, it would still be sticking there to this day! Why? Because I was given such rough measurements – a handful of this, a pinch of that. Obviously someone was trying to keep that recipe secret! Chinese radish is seen as quite a humble vegetable, which is why it is supplemented here with more expensive ingredients such as Chinese mushrooms, dried shrimps and Chinese *lap cheong* sausage to make this dish fit for a celebration. Chinese radish is the perfect accompaniment because it soaks up all those wonderful umami flavours, making this dim sum really special.

MAKES **2 loaves**
PREPARATION TIME **30 minutes**
COOKING TIME **45 minutes, plus 1 hour cooling**

8 dried Chinese mushrooms
3 tablespoons dried shrimp
2 large Chinese radishes (daikon), peeled and grated
3 teaspoons salt
3 tablespoons vegetable oil, plus extra for greasing
3 Chinese sausages (*lap cheong*), diced
2 spring onions, diced
1 tablespoon light soy sauce
1 tablespoon Shaoxing rice wine
1½ teaspoons white pepper
250g rice flour
2 tablespoons wheat starch
2 teaspoons caster sugar
Sweet Chilli Sauce (see page 156), to serve

You will need 2 x 23cm loaf tins, greased with a little vegetable oil

1 Place the Chinese mushrooms and dried shrimps together in a bowl, cover with hot water and set aside to soak for approx. 15 minutes until soft. Drain well, discarding the soaking liquor, and chop into small pieces.

2 Place the grated radish and 2 teaspoons of the salt in a wok and pour over enough water to cover. Bring to the boil over a medium heat and cook for 15 minutes. Drain through a colander set over a bowl or measuring jug to collect the cooking liquid. Measure out 250ml cooking liquid and set aside, discarding the rest.

3 Clean and dry the wok and return it to a high heat with 2 tablespoons of the vegetable oil. Add the diced Chinese sausages, mushrooms, shrimps, spring onions, light soy sauce, Shaoxing wine and 1 teaspoon of the white pepper. Stir-fry for 4–5 minutes or until the sausages are partially crispy.

4 Sift the rice flour and wheat starch into a large bowl and add the drained grated radish and cooked sausage mixture. Season with the remaining 1 teaspoon salt and ½ teaspoon white pepper and the sugar, and stir well with a wooden spoon to combine. Pour in the reserved radish cooking liquid a little at a time and mix to a smooth batter. Divide the mixture between the 2 prepared loaf tins.

5 Fill a wok with water so that it is just over one-quarter full. Set a round cake rack in the centre, cover with a lid and bring to the boil over a high heat. Place the filled tins in a bamboo steamer, reduce the heat to medium and steam the turnip cakes in the wok for 40 minutes.

6 Carefully remove the tins from the steamer and set aside on a wire rack to cool for 60 minutes. Turn out onto a plate and cut into thin slices. To serve, steam the slices for 5 minutes. Alternatively, heat a wok or frying pan over a high heat, add the remaining 1 tablespoon of vegetable oil and pan-fry the slices of cake for 3–4 minutes. Accompany with Sweet Chilli Sauce.

 LISA'S TIP The radish in the loaf tin will release water during steaming. The batter needs to be thick but not too dry. If the radish is too dry, add a little water to the batter.

Taro Cake

香芋糕

Mum explained to me that taro is as hard as stone but, with enough fire, it can be ground down to be soft, squidgy putty in your hands. Taro is a tropical plant and is from the family of root vegetables called Araceae. Taro can often be referred to as yam. It is grown in the paddy fields in China and has a nutty flavour. In its raw form it is toxic because of the calcium oxalate, which can cause kidney stones, but when soaked in cold water and then cooked this toxicity is thankfully minimised and the root is safe to eat.

SERVES **4–6**

PREPARATION TIME **40 minutes, plus overnight soaking**

COOKING TIME **50 minutes, plus cooling and overnight chilling**

600g taro
5 dried Chinese mushrooms
10g dried shrimps
3 dried scallops
1 spring onion, finely diced
2 tablespoons vegetable oil, plus
    extra for greasing
2 Chinese sausages (lap cheong**),**
    cut into 2cm dice
700ml water
1 tablespoon oyster sauce
1 teaspoon chicken stock powder
1 teaspoon caster sugar
1 teaspoon salt
½ teaspoon Chinese five spice
    powder
½ teaspoon white pepper
180g rice flour
50g potato starch
½ teaspoon sesame oil

You will need a 20cm cake tin, greased with a little oil and lined with greaseproof paper

1 Peel the taro, cut it into 5cm cubes and set aside to soak overnight in a bowl of cold water.

2 Place the Chinese mushrooms, dried shrimps, scallops and spring onion in a bowl, cover with hot water and set aside to soak until soft, approx. 15 minutes. Drain well, discarding the soaking liquor, and chop the mushrooms, shrimps and scallops into small pieces.

3 Heat a wok over a high heat with 1 tablespoon of the vegetable oil. Add the Chinese mushrooms, shrimps, scallops, spring onion and diced Chinese sausage and stir-fry for 2 minutes. Set aside.

4 Prepare the flavoured liquids. Combine 350ml water, the oyster sauce, chicken stock powder, sugar, salt, five-spice powder and pepper in a bowl, and mix well to dissolve the stock powder.

5 Drain the soaked taro, discarding the soaking liquor, and add to the wok. Pour over the flavoured liquids mixture from the bowl into the wok and boil for 15 minutes over a high heat until the taro has softened.

6 Meanwhile, combine the rice flour and potato starch in a mixing bowl. Pour in the remaining water, a little at a time, and mix to a smooth, runny batter with no lumps. Add the flour mixture to the taro in the wok and stir continuously for 10 minutes until the batter thickens. Remove the wok from the heat and stir in the sesame oil along with the reserved mushroom and sausage mixture. Spoon into the prepared tin and level the surface with a palette knife.

7 To cook, fill a wok with water so that it is just over one-quarter full. Set a round cake rack in the centre, cover with a lid and bring to the boil over a high heat. Place the cake in a bamboo steamer and reduce the heat to medium. Steam in the wok for 40 minutes. Carefully remove the cake from the steamer and set aside on a wire rack to cool for 1 hour, then transfer the cake, still in its tin, to the fridge to chill overnight.

8 The following day, cut the cake into wedges. Heat the remaining 1 tablespoon of oil in a wok over a medium heat and pan-fry the slices of cake for 3–4 minutes on each side until golden brown. Serve as they are.

 LISA'S TIP If you can't source fresh taro, you can use frozen taro pieces, which are available already peeled. You can freeze the steamed cake in an airtight container, then defrost each portion and pan-fry as above.

Sweets & Desserts

糖果和甜點

Chrysanthemum Pastries
菊花餅

I am still learning about the relationship between food and love, and these beautifully shaped Chrysanthemum Pastries reflect my optimism about first love: traditionally the folds are interwoven roots to cement the relationship, and each petal represents a promise that goes full circle – a bond that will last for eternity.

MAKES **16**
PREPARATION TIME **45 minutes, plus
30 minutes resting time**
COOKING TIME **20 minutes**

**300g sweet potatoes, peeled and
  cut into 4cm chunks**
**10g dried chrysanthemum petals,
  soaked in 30ml hot water**
30g unsalted butter
**50g strawberry jam, plus extra
  to decorate**
30g caster sugar
2 eggs
For the water dough
**200g plain flour, plus extra
  for dusting**
1 tablespoon caster sugar
½ teaspoon vanilla extract
100ml water
50g lard or shortening, cubed
For the oil dough
140g plain flour
85g lard or shortening, cubed

1 Place the sweet potatoes in a pan of boiling water over a high heat for 10 minutes until soft. Drain and tip into a bowl, add the chrysanthemum-infused water, discarding the petals, and mash with a fork until smooth.

2 To make the water dough, sift the flour into a bowl and add the sugar, vanilla extract, water and lard. Mix the ingredients together to form a soft dough, and then turn out onto a floured surface and knead until smooth, approx. 5 minutes. Cover and leave to rest for 10 minutes at room temperature.

3 To make the oil dough, sift the flour into a bowl and add the lard. Mix the ingredients together until they form a soft dough. Cover with clingfilm and transfer to the fridge.

4 Preheat the oven to 200°C/gas 6 and line a baking tray with baking parchment. Add the butter, jam and sugar to the mashed sweet potato and crack in an egg. Mix the ingredients together until thoroughly combined, and then cover the bowl with clingfilm and set aside in the fridge to firm up in the fridge for 20 minutes.

5 Dust a work surface with flour and cut the oil dough and water dough into 16 equal round balls. Flatten the oil dough balls into discs approx. 5cm wide. Place the oil dough balls in the centre of the water dough discs and use your fingers to draw the water dough around the oil dough to form a ball.

6 Using a rolling pin, roll out each dough ball until it is approx. 7cm in length. Roll up the pastry so that it looks like a Swiss roll, then turn the pastry 90 degrees and roll forward into a small round dough ball again. Repeat this process three times. This will help to give the pastry its crisp yet soft texture.

7 After the third roll, shape the dough ball into a round wrapper using a rolling pin to roll it out to a 7cm disc with a thicker centre and a thinner rim.

8 Remove the filling from the fridge and divide it into 16 equal portions. Shape into round balls in the palms of your hands. Place a ball of filling in the centre of each circle of dough, draw up the edges of the dough around the filling to enclose it and squeeze the tips together to seal. The filling should be completely encased in dough. Repeat with the rest of the dough balls and filling to give you 16 filled pastries altogether.

9 To create the flower petals, simply snip 12 little cuts around the outside of the pastry circle – start at 12 o'clock, so that the cuts resemble a clock face, but avoid cutting into the centre (the cuts should be approx. 1cm in length).

10 Beat the remaining egg. Arrange the pastries on the prepared baking tray, brush all over with beaten egg and add a dab of strawberry jam in the centre. Bake for 20 minutes until golden brown. Serve hot from the oven with a cup of Chinese tea.

Egg Custard Tarts
蛋撻

Egg custard tarts are one of the most famous dim sum and a family favourite. When I bite into one it transports me back to my childhood filled with laughter and food. The secret is to use puff pastry to create a flaky case. These are different from Western egg custard tarts because the filling is a lot sweeter and cinnamon is not used.

MAKES **10**
PREPARATION TIME **1 hour, plus**
1 hour chilling time
COOKING TIME **25 minutes**

For the puff pastry
120g unsalted butter, chilled
220g plain flour, plus extra
   for dusting
1 teaspoon caster sugar
½ teaspoon salt
20g unsalted butter, softened,
   plus extra for greasing
100ml water
For the filling
3 medium eggs
250ml semi-skimmed milk
100g caster sugar
3 teaspoons evaporated milk
½ teaspoon vanilla extract

You will need 10 dariole moulds and
a 7cm pastry cutter

1 Slice the chilled butter into even rectangles. Lay a large sheet of clingfilm on a work surface and arrange the butter on top in 3 rows of 3. Fold the clingfilm over the butter and transfer the whole lot to the freezer to firm up for 10 minutes.

2 Remove the butter from the freezer. Keep the butter wrapped in the clingfilm. Using a rolling pin, roll out the butter so that it merges into one piece, approx. 15 x 15cm. Return to the freezer to firm up while you prepare the dough.

3 Sift the flour into a large bowl and add the sugar, salt and softened butter. Pour in the water a little at a time and mix to a firm but pliable dough. Turn out the dough onto a floured work surface and knead briefly until smooth. Return the dough to the bowl, cover with clingfilm and set aside to rest in the fridge for 30 minutes.

4 Meanwhile, make the filling. Beat the eggs together in a bowl. Place the milk and sugar in a small saucepan and stir over a medium heat for 3–4 minutes to dissolve the sugar. Pour the hot milk over the beaten eggs and whisk together. Add the evaporated milk and vanilla extract and whisk again. Cover the bowl with clingfilm and transfer the filling to the fridge to chill for 1 hour.

5 Grease 10 dariole moulds with butter. Dust a work surface with flour and roll out the dough into a long rectangle, approx. 30cm x 20cm. Remove the butter from the freezer and peel back the clingfilm from one side. Place the butter in the centre of the dough and peel off the other side of clingfilm. Fold the left-hand side of the dough over the butter, then the right-hand side, then fold up the bottom and fold down the top to form a parcel. Place the dough in a plastic bag and transfer it to the freezer to firm up for 10 minutes.

6 Remove the dough from the freezer and roll it out again to form a rectangle, approx. 30cm x 20cm. Fold the left-hand side of the dough to the centre, then the right-hand side, then fold up the bottom and fold down the top to form a parcel. Return the dough to the plastic bag and transfer it to the freezer to firm up for 10 minutes.

7 Repeat the rolling, folding and freezing process 3 more times.

8 Preheat the oven to 220°C/gas 7. To prepare the pastry cases, roll out the pastry to a thickness of 1cm. Stamp out 10 rounds using a 7cm pastry cutter and insert one in each of the dariole moulds. Pour the chilled egg custard into the moulds so that they are just over three-quarters full – to leave room for the custard to rise. Place the filled moulds on a baking tray and transfer them to the oven to cook for 15 minutes, then reduce the temperature to 180°C/gas 4 and cook for a further 5 minutes. Turn off the oven and leave the custards inside for a further 5 minutes until they are fully set. To serve, remove the tarts from their cases and accompany with Jasmine tea.

Turtle-shaped Pastries with Red Bean Paste

紅龜糕

When I close my eyes, I'm transported back to the Caribbean, where I spent some of my most adventurous and carefree days. The Cayman Islands have a famous turtle farm and, in honour of the land of sunshine, I'm making these turtle-shaped pastries for the friends who made me so welcome during my stay. I can still feel the warmth of the white sands between my toes at Rum Point – where the stingrays swim in the turquoise waters, kissing my toes as I slurp on a Mississippi Mudslide Cocktail. Here's a little piece of that paradise.

MAKES **8 turtles**
PREPARATION TIME **20 minutes, plus
1 hour and 20 minutes resting time**
COOKING TIME **20 minutes**

**500g plain flour, plus extra
  for dusting**
50g caster sugar
2 teaspoons dried yeast
1½ teaspoons salt
150ml lukewarm water
150ml lukewarm semi-skimmed milk
**70g unsalted butter, melted, plus
  extra for brushing**
200g red bean paste
black sesame seeds, to decorate

1 Preheat the oven to 200°C/gas 6 and line a baking tray with baking parchment.

2 Sift the flour into a large bowl, add the sugar, yeast, salt and water and mix together with a wooden spoon to form a stiff dough. Cover the bowl with clingfilm and set aside in a warm place for 20 minutes until you see bubbles appear in the mixture.

3 Add the milk and melted butter and mix together with a wooden spoon until the mixture comes together into a dough. Turn out onto a floured work surface and knead until smooth, approx. 5 minutes. Return the dough to the bowl, cover with clingfilm and set aside in a warm place to rise for 1 hour until the dough has doubled in size.

4 Meanwhile, divide the red bean paste into 8 equal portions and shape into balls. Set aside.

5 Dust a work surface with flour and roll out the dough into a 40cm log shape. Apportion one-third of the dough for the head and feet of the turtle. Cut the remaining log into 8 even pieces, which will form the turtle's body, and shape into balls in the palms of your hands. Using your thumb, make an indent in each dough ball and insert a ball of red bean paste into each. Draw up the dough around the red bean paste to enclose it fully and squeeze together at the tip to seal. Turn the filled dough balls upside down so the smooth part becomes the turtle's shell.

6 Use the remaining dough to form smaller dough balls for the head and tiny dough balls for the feet.

7 Assemble the turtles' body, head and legs by brushing the joints with melted butter and pressing them together. Insert two black sesame seeds in the face to form the turtles' eyes.

8 Arrange the finished turtles on the prepared baking tray and bake for 20 minutes until golden brown. Serve hot straight out of the oven.

 LISA'S TIP To attach the head and legs to the turtle's body you can also use beaten egg if you don't want to use melted butter.

Chocolate-coated Coconut Macaroons

巧克力和椰香馬卡龍

The nickname for these coconut macaroons is 'grinning faces' based on the three little eyes on the coconut base. Coconut is classed as a fruit but often confused with being a nut; it's actually a one-seeded drupe – with water, milk, flesh, sugar and oil. Palm trees produce coconuts up to 13 times a year and, although it takes a year for the coconuts to mature, a fully blossomed tree can produce between 60 and 180 coconuts in a single harvest. Coconuts are highly nutritious and rich in fibre, vitamins C, E, B1, B3, B5 and B6 as well as minerals including iron, selenium, sodium, calcium, magnesium and phosphorus.

MAKES **12**
PREPARATION TIME **1 hour**
COOKING TIME **20 minutes, plus
cooling and 20 minutes chilling time**

1 large egg white
160ml condensed milk
2 teaspoons vanilla extract
1/4 teaspoon salt
300g desiccated coconut
**400g dark chocolate (approx.
   70 per cent cocoa solids), chopped**
1 teaspoon unsalted butter

1 Preheat the oven to 160°C/gas 3 and place an oven rack in the bottom third of the oven. Line a baking tray with baking parchment.
2 Combine the egg white, condensed milk, vanilla and salt in a mixing bowl. Whisk until the whites and sugar are completely combined and the mixture is frothy, approx. 7 minutes. Scatter the coconut over the egg white mixture and stir until the coconut is evenly moistened.
3 With wet hands to prevent sticking, shape the coconut mixture into 12 small balls, approx. 4cm in diameter. Arrange on the prepared baking tray, spacing them 3cm apart to allow room for them to spread. Bake in the bottom third of the oven for 20 minutes until they are golden brown and the ball has spread slightly.
4 Remove the macaroons from the oven and leave to cool on the baking tray for 5 minutes before transferring them to a wire rack to cool completely.
5 Once the macaroons are cooled completely (approx. 30 minutes), line 2 baking trays with baking parchment.
6 Melt the chocolate and butter in a small heatproof bowl set over a pan of almost-simmering water, stirring once or twice, until smooth. Remove from the heat.
7 Coat each macaroon by dipping the base in the melted chocolate. Scrape off the excess chocolate and place the completed macaroon on the prepared baking trays.
8 Transfer the macaroons to the fridge for 20 minutes or until the chocolate sets. Store in an airtight container for up to a week.

LISA'S TIP To melt the chocolate uniformly, it's important to stir it in a bain-marie and to keep the water just below simmering. Adding the butter will make the chocolate more glossy. Make sure you don't splash water into the chocolate or else it will seize and harden. This is caused by the sugar crystals in the chocolate getting wet, making them clump together. Alternatively, you can melt the chocolate in the microwave. This will depend on your wattage but melt it a minute at a time until the chocolate has melted completely.

Almond Cookies

My strongest childhood memories are of playing a game with my sisters in the kitchen where we would dare each other to run to the kitchen counter, which was head and shoulders taller than us, and stretch out a fat hand to reach for the plate of freshly baked almond cookies. The prize was sweet, but if Mum caught us we'd forfeit dessert and treats for a week for being disobedient and greedy. The rule was that we had to wait until after dinner to enjoy an almond cookie, but for me that was torture and it was worth the risk to acquire one commando-style.

MAKES **16**
PREPARATION TIME **20 minutes**
COOKING TIME **10 minutes, plus cooling**

200g margarine
100g caster sugar
2 medium eggs
1 tablespoon almond extract
300g plain flour, plus extra
   for dusting
¼ teaspoon salt
½ teaspoon baking powder
To decorate
70g blanched almonds, halved
1 beaten egg, to glaze

1 Preheat the oven to 220°C/gas 7 and line a baking tray with baking parchment.
2 Put the margarine and sugar in a bowl and whisk together until pale and fluffy. Add the eggs a little at a time and continue whisking. Add the almond extract and whisk again.
3 Sift the flour into a second mixing bowl and add the salt and baking powder. Pour in the egg mixture and mix with a wooden spoon to form a firm dough.
4 Turn out the dough onto a floured surface and divide into two equal portions. Roll out to form two log shapes and cut each one into 8 even pieces.
5 Shape into 16 balls in the palms of your hands and arrange on the prepared baking tray, spacing them apart. Flatten each ball with your fingers and place an almond half in the centre of each. Brush with beaten egg to glaze and bake for 10 minutes until pale golden brown. Serve with Jasmine tea.

 LISA'S TIP You can use a fork to score the edges of the cookies before baking. It will make a lovely pattern on them.

Chinese-style Doughnuts

中式甜甜圈

This is my take on the Youtiao, also known as the salty Chinese doughnut, which literally translated means 'oil-fried devil'. The story behind the name dates back to the Song Dynasty, which was governed by a general called Yue Fei who was brought down by a man named Qin Hui and his wife. The people found this unjust and ate these doughnuts in protest at the 'oil-fried devils'. The savoury version is made with two strands of dough to represent the traitorous husband and wife. In savoury form these doughnuts are made into a long, golden brown, deep-fried strips of dough normally eaten in China at breakfast as an accompaniment to rice congee. In this recipe I have adapted them, including sugar and making them bite-sized so that they make a perfect dessert.

MAKES **15**

PREPARATION TIME **30 minutes, plus**
1 hour resting time

COOKING TIME **10 minutes**

440ml semi-skimmed milk

100g unsalted butter, melted

125g caster sugar

4 eggs, beaten

2 teaspoons fast-action dried yeast

600g plain flour

250ml vegetable oil, for deep-frying

397g tin condensed milk

50g icing sugar, for dusting

1 Pour the milk into a medium saucepan and warm over a gentle heat. Pour the milk into a large bowl and add the melted butter and 75g of the sugar and mix well. Add the eggs and mix well, then add the yeast and stir into the mixture, which will start foaming as the yeast reacts with the warm liquids.

2 Sift the plain flour into a separate large bowl, and make a well in the centre. Pour the wet mixture into the flour and stir to combine into a thick batter. Cover the bowl with clingfilm and set aside to rise in a warm place for 1 hour until the dough has doubled in size.

3 Heat the oil to 180°C in a wok or deep saucepan over a high heat and fill with the vegetable oil (to test the temperature, see page 149). Scoop some of the batter in your hand and, using the gap between your thumb and index finger, squeeze out a ball of dough approx. the size of 2 grapes. Add to the hot oil and cook for 4–5 minutes. Using a Chinese wire net or slotted spoon, scoop out the fried doughnuts and leave to drain on kitchen paper. Cook the remaining doughnuts in batches.

5 Transfer the cooked doughnuts to a plate and gradually drizzle over the condensed milk, then sprinkle with the remaining caster and the icing sugar. Serve hot. They will be light and moreish.

 LISA'S TIP When cooking with hot oil it's important to drop the ball of dough carefully into the hot oil. Drop the dough close to the oil so the oil does not splash back on you.

Pineapple Buns

菠蘿包

There is no actual pineapple in these buns, but they are named so because of the pineapple colour of the sweet crust. Our grandmother used to roll her eyes when she saw a family friend, nicknamed 'Uncle Dog', walk up the drive to her house. He was given that nickname because he was always being chased through the neighbourhood by a little dog, which he was petrified of. This particular dog could smell fear and pork chops, and Uncle Dog always seemed to be carrying a bag of pork chops. So, as night follows day, the little dog would go after him and the chase would ensue in cartoon-slapstick fashion with Uncle Dog ultimately throwing the bag of pork chops as far as he could to divert the little dog. Our grandmother often had arguments with Uncle Dog, because he would always come to visit just as dinner was almost ready and she would call him a 'pineapple bun', which in Chinese slang meant he was a stingy bugger who wouldn't pay for anything. I'm not quite sure how an innocent pineapple bun got that unfavourable reputation, but if you look at the topping of this dim sum it doesn't quite cover the entire bun …

MAKES **12**

PREPARATION TIME **1 hour, plus**
1½ hours resting time
COOKING TIME **35 minutes**

For the buns
3 teaspoons dried yeast
3½ teaspoons caster sugar
150ml warm semi-skimmed milk
1 egg yolk
30g unsalted butter, melted
360g plain flour, plus extra
  for dusting
½ teaspoon salt
For the topping
2 teaspoons semi-skimmed milk
2 egg yolks
50g unsalted butter (at room
  temperature), cut into pieces
2 teaspoons baking powder
80g caster sugar
3 teaspoons honey
140g plain flour
For the glaze
2 egg yolks, beaten with 5 teaspoons
  milk

1 Preheat the oven to 180°C/gas 4 and line a baking tray with baking parchment.
2 Put the yeast, sugar and milk in a bowl and whisk together. Set aside at room temperature for 15 minutes to allow the yeast to become frothy.
3 Add the egg yolk and melted butter and whisk thoroughly until combined.
4 Sift the flour into a second bowl and add the salt. Add the yeast mixture a little at a time and mix with a wooden spoon to a soft dough. Turn out the dough onto a floured work surface and knead until smooth, approx. 5 minutes. Return the dough to the bowl, cover with clingfilm and set aside in a warm place to rise for 1 hour until doubled in size.
5 Knock back the dough with your fists, turn it out onto a floured work surface and knead briefly for 5 minutes. Return the dough to the bowl, cover with a damp tea towel and set aside to prove for 30 minutes.
6 Separate the dough into 12 even pieces and roll into balls in the palms of your hands. Arrange on a work surface and cover with a damp cloth while you prepare the topping.
7 To make the dough topping, whisk together the milk and egg yolks in a bowl. Add the butter, baking powder, sugar and honey and whisk together. Gradually incorporate the flour and mix to a smooth dough. Turn out the dough onto your work surface and roll into a log shape. Cut into 12 even pieces and shape into balls. Using a rolling pin, roll out each piece of topping into a circle, approx. 10cm in diameter.
8 To assemble the buns, lay the circles of topping over the dough balls and brush with beaten egg to glaze. Arrange the finished buns on the prepared baking tray and bake for 30 minutes. The pineapple buns will have expanded and the crust will be golden brown. Reduce the temperature to 160°C/gas 3 and bake for a further 2 minutes until the crust is crispy. Serve hot with a cup of oolong tea.

Sweet Custard Cream Buns

奶黃包

Although these have a more doughy texture than doughnuts, they are equally delicious and light. The custard filling gives them a gentle hint of sweetness but isn't overly sweet like jam. There is something utterly endearing about these dim sum buns, which could be made as a gift, as an alternative for a birthday, as a wedding cake tower, or just as an indulgent treat to be enjoyed by yourself. I believe you will be thoroughly warmed when you first make them – they are certainly something seen less frequently on dim sum menus and therefore, in my opinion, are quite special.

MAKES **15 buns**
PREPARATION TIME **30 minutes, plus
1 hour to prove and 15 minutes to rest**
COOKING TIME **10 minutes**

For the dough
8g dried yeast
100ml warm water
225g plain flour
1 egg white
60g sugar
25g lard
½ teaspoon white vinegar
For the filling
150g caster sugar
60g cornflour
20g plain flour
2 eggs
½ teaspoon vanilla extract
75ml condensed milk
300ml water
50g unsalted butter, melted
40g custard powder

1 Add the yeast into the warm water and stir. Set aside.
2 Sift the flour into a large bowl. Add the egg white, sugar, lard and white vinegar and then the yeast mixture to the bowl. Mix with a wooden spoon until it comes together to form a dough. On a lightly floured work surface, knead the dough for 10 minutes until it is a smooth texture. Place the dough in a bowl, cover with clingfilm and set aside to rise for 1 hour.
3 To make the filling, combine the sugar, cornflour and plain flour in a medium bowl. Add the eggs, vanilla extract, condensed milk, water, butter and custard powder and stir until the mixture has no more lumps and is quite thick. Fill a wok full with one-quarter water and bring to the boil. Place a bamboo steamer on top. Place the bowl of custard mixture in the bamboo steamer and steam over a high heat for 15minutes until the mixture is just firm. Don't overcook the filling or it will become too hard in texture.
4 Once the filling is fluffy and moist, remove from the steamer and allow to cool slightly. While it is still warm and malleable, break it up and shape it into small balls either by hand or using 2 teaspoons
5 When the dough has doubled in size, knead it and roll it out into a log shape. Divide the dough into 15 pieces and roll eachout into a small ball approx. 5cm wide. Place them on a baking tray and cover with a damp tea towel. Leave to rise for 15 minutes.
6 Using the palm of your hand, flatten the ball of dough into a round disc. Place a ball of custard filling in the centre, approx. 1 heaped tablespoon. Bring the edges to the centre and seal the bun by pinching the edge at the tip.
7 Heat the wok one-quarter full of water and place the bamboo steamer lined with parchment inside on a rack. When boiling, reduce the heat and place the buns in the bamoo steamer. Steam over a medium heat for 10 minutes. Serve hot with a cup of Chinese tea.

 LISA'S TIP These buns can be frozen to eat at a later date. Cool the buns, transfer to an airtight container and put in the freezer. To cook from frozen, steam for 15 minutes over a medium heat.

Chocolate Swiss Roll
巧克力瑞士卷

I know this dim sum doesn't sound very Chinese, but if you go to any Chinese supermarket you will find the shelves filled with these delicious chocolate Swiss rolls. The texture and taste is quite different from the type you buy from a mainstream supermarket – this one is a lighter version and much springier. It's not the easiest recipe to make, but I always feel a sense of accomplishment when I bake it. This dessert is a family favourite and a lot of fun for kids to get involved with. Whenever we make this, it's a messy day filled with laughter and love. Oh, and extra chocolate please.

SERVES 4
PREPARATION TIME **30 minutes**
COOKING TIME **30 minutes**

120g egg yolks
95g caster sugar
35g honey
160g egg whites
15g cocoa powder
50g plain flour
20g unsalted butter, melted
35ml semi-skimmed milk
For the filling
150g whipping cream
100g dark chocolate, melted
1 tablespoon caster sugar

You will need a Swiss roll tin
25 x 35cm

1 Preheat the oven to 200°C/gas 6 and line a Swiss roll tin with baking parchment. Combine the egg yolks, 35g of the sugar and the honey in a heatproof bowl and set over a saucepan of gently simmering water. Using an electric whisk, whisk continuously for 8 minutes until the mixture is very warm approx. 40°C. Carefully remove the bowl from the pan and continue to whisk for a further 10 minutes until the mixture becomes pale and very thick.

2 In a separate bowl, whisk the egg whites until they form stiff peaks. Add half the egg whites to the batter and fold in carefully with a large metal spoon.

3 Sift the cocoa powder and flour into the batter mixture and add the remaining 60g sugar. Fold in carefully with a metal spoon until fully combined. Add the remaining egg whites and mix in gently. Add the melted butter and milk and stir to combine.

4 Pour the batter into the prepared Swiss roll tin and tap the tin to ensure it is evenly distributed. Bake for 30 minutes until springy to the touch, then remove from the oven.

5 While the sponge is warm, lay a sheet of baking parchment over the chocolate cake and turn it upside down. Carefully peel off the baking parchment from the bottom of the cake.

6 Score a line along the bottom of the sponge, approx. 2.5cm away from the edge on one short side, then roll up the Swiss roll from the scored end. Leave to cool.

7 Melt the chocolate and butter in a small heatproof bowl set over a pan of almost-simmering water, stirring once or twice, until smooth. Remove from the heat.

8 To make the chocolate filling, whip the cream until it forms soft peaks. Add the melted chocolate and sugar and mix together using a spatula until completely smooth.

9 To assemble the Swiss Roll gently unroll the sponge once it is cool. Spoon the chocolate cream filling evenly over the surface of the sponge leaving a 4cm gap from the edges. Spread the chocolate cream over the surface using a palette knife.

10 Push the paper towards you and ease the sponge over the filling. Roll all the way to the end then turn over to seal the filling. Chill in the fridge for 1 hour. To serve, cut the Swiss roll into 2cm slices and accompany with Jasmine tea.

 LISA'S TIP Always roll a Swiss roll when it is just out of the oven and still pliable. Don't overfill the Swiss roll with filling as it will be hard to roll and very messy.

Steamed Sponge Cake
蒸馬來糕

Dim sum also includes many sweet cakes and buns and this is one of the most popular offerings on the sweets list. There is nothing quite so satisfying as biting into a hot sponge cake that has literally just come out of the steamer. I had a childhood friend whose mum made the most amazing steamed sponge cake. I remember how we would count down the minutes together before we could lift the lid – it was forbidden, absolutely strictly forbidden to open the steamer before the time was up! That is the trick, to wait, and your patience will be rewarded.

SERVES **4**
PREPARATION TIME **20 minutes, plus**
40 minutes resting
COOKING TIME **40 minutes**

240g plain flour
50g custard powder
2 teaspoons baking powder
2 teaspoons bicarbonate of soda
6 medium eggs
300g brown sugar
10g lard, melted, plus extra
   for greasing
1 teaspoon vanilla extract
1 teaspoon Cointreau
2 teaspoons orange zest

You will need a 20cm round cake tin

1 Grease and line a 20cm round cake tin with baking parchment. Sift the flour, custard powder, baking powder and bicarbonate soda into a large bowl. mix together until fully combined with no lumps.

2 Crack the eggs into a separate bowl and whisk together using an electric whisk until pale and frothy. Gradually add the sugar and beat until smooth and light. Add this to the dry ingredients and mix well. Cover and set aside to rest for 30 minutes.

3 Add the melted lard and vanilla extract, Cointreau and orange zest and mix well. Leave to rest for a further 10 minutes.

4 Pour the batter into the prepared cake tin. Fill a wok with water so that it is just over one-quarter full. Set a round cake rack in the centre, cover with a lid and bring to the boil over a high heat. Place the cake inside a bamboo steamer on top of the wok and steam over a high heat for 40 minutes. Remove from the heat and leave the cake in the steamer for 1 minute with the lid slightly ajar.

5 Slice the hot cake into generous slices and serve with a cup of coffee.

 LISA'S TIP Do not cover the cake with aluminium foil as you want the air to circulate to cook the steamed cake.

Sweet Mandarin Pudding Cake

香橙布丁蛋糕

This is our signature dish and our mum says it is a twist on trifle – a nod to our British upbringing but incorporating our restaurant's namesake by using mandarin juice. It is a great recipe for celebrations and very easy to make. The tartness of the mandarin juice lifts this sponge cake and packs a punch of healthy vitamin C.

SERVES **6**

PREPARATION TIME **20 minutes, plus 50 minutes chilling time**

300ml semi-skimmed milk

2½ teaspoons agar-agar powder

100g caster sugar

300ml mandarin juice

zest of 1 orange

2 egg yolks

20g custard powder

1 teaspoon butter

1 teaspoon orange food colouring (natural)

15cm square vanilla sponge cake to fit the size of the jelly mould

You will need a 15cm jelly mould

1 Pour the milk into a saucepan, add the agar-agar powder and sugar and bring to the boil over a high heat. Cook for 10 minutes, stirring all the time, until thick. Remove from the heat and add the mandarin juice, orange zest, egg yolks, custard powder, butter and orange food colouring.

2 Pour the mixture into a jelly mould. Cool, then transfer to the fridge to chill for 50 minutes until set.

3 Once the pudding has set, layer the sponge cake over the surface in one piece to make a two-tier dessert.

4 To serve, invert the pudding onto a plate and remove the mould so that the sponge cake is sitting underneath the pudding. Serve with some whipped cream, accompanied by green tea.

Coconut Acai Berry Crumble

蘋果西莓椰汁酥餅

This is a crumble with a difference because it contains acai berry juice. These deep purple berries originate from the Amazon and taste of fruity red wine with a hint of chocolate – making them perfect as a dessert. They can be bought dried, frozen, or fresh, as a juice, and this recipe works best with the juice. Within the nutritious pulp and skin, acai berries are packed with antioxidants, amino acids, fibre, essential fatty acids, vitamins and minerals, making them a near perfect energising fruit. The antioxidants found in acai berries, anthocyanins, are excellent for heart health. And this dessert is delicious too.

MAKES **4**
PREPARATION TIME **20 minutes**
COOKING TIME **20–25 minutes**

For the topping
300g plain flour
1 teaspoon salt
170g brown sugar
200g unsalted butter, chilled,
  cut into pieces, plus 2 teaspoons
30g caster sugar
30g desiccated coconut
50g rolled oats
For the fruit
400g Bramley apples
100ml acai berry juice
2–3 tablespoons caster sugar
zest of 1 orange

You will need a 24cm ovenproof dish
or four 10cm ramekins

1 Preheat the oven to 200°C/gas 6. First prepare the topping. Sift the flour into a bowl, add the salt and brown sugar and rub in the 200g butter with your fingertips until the mixture resembles breadcrumbs. Stir in the caster sugar, desiccated coconut and oats and mix well.

2 Peel and thickly slice the apples. Put in a bowl with the acai berry juice and toss with the sugar and orange zest. Tip the fruit into a 24cm ovenproof dish or divide between 4 x 10cm ramekins.

3 Cover the fruit with the crumble topping and dot the surface with the 2 teaspoons of butter. Bake for 20–25 minutes until the topping is golden and crisp. Serve warm with custard or clotted cream.

LISA'S TIP When rubbing in the crumble mixture make sure you lift up your mixture to allow the large pieces of butter to be broken down.

Tofu Far

豆腐花

Tofu is to the Chinese what cheese is to the French, a national treasure. Prince Liu An, the grandson of Emperor Liu Bang, was first credited with its discovery during the Han Dynasty. Legend has it that he went off to the mountains in search of immortal elixirs that would make him live forever, but instead he discovered a pile of white and tender soft layers of tofu. Tofu is bland and can absorb any flavour. Here it is accompanied with ginger syrup, which imparts elements of heat and sweetness.

SERVES **4**

PREPARATION TIME **20 minutes, plus 1 hour chilling time**

COOKING TIME 1**5 minutes, plus cooling time**

75ml water

7g packet of gelatine powder

1 litre soya milk

40g caster sugar

For the ginger syrup

150g soft light brown sugar

30 thin strips of fresh root ginger

150ml water

½ teaspoon salt

1 Add the water to a small bowl and sprinkle the gelatine over the surface, whisking with a fork. Stand the bowl in a larger bowl of hot water and set aside for 10 minutes, stirring occasionally until the gelatine dissolves.

2 Put the soya milk and sugar in a medium saucepan and stir over a high heat for 10 minutes until the sugar has dissolved in the liquid. Reduce the heat to low and whisk in the dissolved gelatine. Mix fast to ensure the gelatine is thoroughly incorporated into the warm soya milk. Strain the mixture through a sieve into a shallow metal container, the cool and set aside in the fridge for 1 hour until set.

3 To make the ginger syrup, put the light brown sugar, ginger and water in a pan over a high heat and boil rapidly for 5 minutes until the sugar dissolves and the syrup darkens slightly. Add the salt, and then remove the ginger syrup from the heat. Set aside to cool and thicken.

4 To serve, use a large cooking spoon to place 2–3 slices of the tofu far onto a plate. Add 5 tablespoons of the ginger syrup over each portion and serve.

Chrysanthemum Tea & Lychee Jellies

荔枝菊花茶凍糕

Our grandmother told me that when she was growing up in Guangzhou, the sky was so clear you could see all the stars. She said this dim sum reminded her of her childhood – lying side by side with her sisters, each wishing on a star that their lives would have meaning and purpose. In the 1920s, girls in China had very little value – only boys counted. Their wishes must have been heard, as their father treated my grandmother and her five sisters with much love and he respected them as much as he would have done had they been sons.

Chrysanthemum tea is known to be an excellent thirst quencher because of its "cooling" properties which means it lowers body heat - perfect for the scorching summer months in China. This dessert with lychees is also perfect for the summer because there are so many lychees growing on the trees!

SERVES **4–6**

PREPARATION TIME **20 minutes, plus 2 hours chilling time**

COOKING TIME **10 minutes**

30g dried chrysanthemum tea leaves

250ml boiling water

10g konnyaku powder (or 2 tablespoons gelatine powder)

60g caster sugar

50ml fresh lychee juice

425g tin lychees, drained and chopped into small pieces

1 First make the chrysanthemum tea by mixing the chrysanthemum tea leaves and boiling water in a small bowl. Set aside for 10 minutes to release the flavour. Drain and discard the tea leaves.

2 If using gelatine, whisk with 3 tablespoons water in a bowl. Stand the bowl in a larger bowl of hot water and set aside for 10 minutes, stirring occasionally, until the gelatine dissolves.

3 Place the chrysanthemum tea, sugar and lychee juice in a medium saucepan and warm over a medium heat until the sugar has dissolved in the liquid. Add the konnyaku powder (or the dissolved gelatine) and stir continuously until the mixture comes to the boil. Remove from the heat.

4 Pour the jelly into a 28 x 18 x 5cm shallow baking tray and scatter over the chopped lychee pieces. Set aside to cool, and then transfer the jelly to the fridge to chill for 2 hours.

5 Slice the jelly into 2.5cm cubes and serve accompanied by Lemon and Ginseng Iced Tea (see page 154).

 LISA'S TIP You could pour the jelly mixture into jelly moulds of different shapes instead of making cubes, if you wish.

Peanut Mochi Balls

花生糯米糍

My family love these Peanut Mochi Balls which we make for Chinese New Year or whenever we fancy a sweet dessert. They are delicious steamed rice flour balls filled with peanuts, sugar and sesame seeds. Other fillings can also be used, such as ice cream, red bean paste and black sesame seeds.

MAKES **16**
PREPARATION TIME **40 minutes**
COOKING TIME **30 minutes**

200g slightly toasted peanuts, finely chopped
350g desiccated coconut
100g sesame seeds
80g caster sugar
For the wrappers
20g rice flour
150g glutinous rice flour
10g instant custard powder
200ml skimmed milk
200ml coconut milk
70g caster sugar
1 tablespoon vegetable oil, plus extra for greasing

1 To make the wrappers, sift the rice flour, glutinous rice flour and custard power into a bowl.

2 Combine the milk, coconut milk, sugar and oil in a saucepan and bring to the boil over a high heat. Reduce the heat and simmer for 5 minutes.

3 Pour the hot milk mixture over the flour mixture and mix to a stiff dough. Place the dough in a greased heatproof bowl. Fill a wok with water so that it is just over one-quarter full. Set a round cake rack in the centre, cover with a lid and bring to the boil over a high heat. Place the heatproof bowl inside a bamboo steamer on top of the wok and steam for 20 minutes. Remove from the steamer and set aside to cool.

4 To make the peanut filling, combine the peanuts, 150g desiccated coconut, sesame seeds and sugar in a bowl and set aside.

5 Turn the dough out onto a work surface and divide into 16 equal portions. Roll into round balls in the palms of your hand. Flatten each ball and roll out to a circle, approx. 8cm in diameter, using a rolling pin.

6 Place 1 heaped tablespoon of peanut filling in the centre of each wrapper and draw up the dough around the sides to enclose the filling. Mould into a ball. Repeat with the rest of the dough and filling to form 16 balls.

7 Dip the mochi balls in water and then roll them in a plate of the remaining desiccated coconut, coating them on all sides, and arrange in standard cupcake cases. Serve.

 LISA'S TIP Always keep the mochi pastry covered because it will dry out quite quickly. Alternatively, if it is too dry, drop some water on it and rework it. This will help seal the mochi ball too.

Green Tea Ice Cream

抹茶冰淇淋

When I first came across this dessert at Anuga, the world's largest food and drinks fair, it was really quite exciting. Tea is one of those ingredients you'd never expect would work with ice cream, but this combination really works – and the beauty is that this recipe is very easy to make. Matcha green tea has a distinct flavour and infuses the ice cream with a beautiful pastel green colour. Tastewise, a small amount goes a long way, as the flavour is very intense. I could imagine it also works well in milkshakes.

SERVES **4**
PREPARATION TIME **20 minutes, plus
freezing time**
COOKING TIME **10 minutes**

3 tablespoons hot water
**1 tablespoon matcha green tea
  powder**
2 egg yolks
50g caster sugar
200ml semi-skimmed milk
200ml double cream

1 Mix the hot water and green tea powder together in a small bowl and set aside. To make the custard base, whisk the egg yolks with the sugar in a medium heavy-based saucepan off the heat. Add the milk, a little at a time, and mix to a smooth paste.
2 Place the pan over a high heat and cook for about 10 minutes, stirring constantly until the custard thickens. Transfer the pan to a sink filled with cold water to rapidly cool the custard.
3 Meanwhile, whip the cream in a bowl until soft peaks form.
4 Add the green tea mixture and the whipped cream to the custard base and stir until thoroughly combined.
5 Pour the mixture into an ice-cream maker and freeze according to the manufacturer's instructions. (Alternatively, pour the mixture into a metal container and freeze until set.)
6 Serve the ice cream in scoops or as part of the Green Tea Mochi Ice Cream Balls (see page 146).

LISA'S TIP In case you were wondering, Japanese green tea leaves are not the same as matcha green tea powder. However, the matcha green tea powder can be turned into a hot green tea by adding hot water.

Green Tea Ice Cream Mochi Balls

綠茶冰淇淋糯米糍

It was a crowded room – an awards function – and the servers were dishing out these beautiful desserts, which I had to try. Just as I bit into one I saw a familiar face I would have recognised anywhere. I'd not seen him in ages and he looked exactly the same as the last time I had seen him years ago. He was Mr Fan, the first chef to teach me how to cook dim sum professionally. A lump stuck in my throat – and then I realised I hadn't finished eating my green tea ice cream mochi ball. He put his hand out and I shook it formally. Behind the fine clothes and smile I was transported back to our first day in the kitchen where I was probably the most awkward and nervous student. We were interrupted by the server, who asked whether we wanted another green tea ice cream mochi ball. I accepted. 'You should make them,' Mr Fan replied, 'You know you can cook anything you want. You have always been a confident cook – even if your personality has taken some time to catch up with your skill. Remember that no one can take away your skill. I am proud of you.' I nodded and smiled back in thanks for his guidance all those years ago.

MAKES **8**

PREPARATION TIME **45 minutes, plus 30 minutes chilling time**

FREEZING TIME **90 minutes**

150g glutinous rice flour

20g rice flour

10g custard powder

200ml skimmed milk

200ml coconut milk

70g caster sugar

1 tablespoon vegetable oil, plus extra for greasing

potato starch, for dusting

Green Tea Ice Cream (see page 145)

You will need 2 baking trays, approx. 28 x 18 x 5 cm

1 To make the mochi dough, sift the glutinous rice flour, rice flour and custard powder into a bowl.

2 Put the milk, coconut milk, sugar and oil in a saucepan over a high heat and bring to the boil. Reduce the heat and simmer for 5 minutes. Slowly add the liquid to the bowl of dry ingredients and mix well until thoroughly combined into a dough. Grease a bowl with a little oil, add the dough and place the bowl inside a bamboo steamer.

3 Fill a wok with water so that it is just over one-quarter full. Set a round cake rack in the centre, cover with a lid and bring to the boil over a high heat. Place the steamer inside the wok and steam for 20 minutes.

4 Sprinkle potato starch over the baking trays. Pour the cooked mochi dough onto the tray and sprinkle some potato starch over the top. Using your hand, press out the mochi so that it becomes evenly spread into a thin layer about the same size as the baking tray (approx. 15 x 30cm). Cool, then transfer the mochi dough to the fridge to chill for 30 minutes.

5 Remove the mochi dough from the fridge and divide it into 8 equal pieces. The easiest way to do this is to divide the dough in half, and then divide each half into 4 pieces. Brush the excess potato starch off both sides of the mocha wrappers. Stack up the wrappers in between layers of clingfilm to prevent them from sticking together and transfer to the freezer to firm up for 1 hour.

6 To make the ice cream mochi, place a piece of clingfilm over a small cup. Starting with the first wrapper, place a ball of ice cream in the centre of the wrapper and then press it into the cup. Draw up the wrapper around the ice cream, using the clingfilm to help mould it into a ball. Use a clean clothes peg to seal the clingfilm, and then transfer the finished ice cream mochi ball to the freezer immediately. Make up the remaining balls in the same way. Serve the green tea mochi balls on a plate.

Sesame Balls with Red Bean Filling

煎堆

As I watched these dim sum bobbing around in the hot oil I realised some had overcooked and I'd slightly burnt the first batch. Should I throw them away, I asked myself, being the perfectionist I am? But I took a bite and they were still delicious – OK aesthetically not that good, but tastewise they were lovely and sweet. As I bit into one, the realisation dawned on me: we've all got many layers – some a bit crunchy like the sesame seeds, some smooth like the pastry, but inside we can all be sweet.

MAKES **12 balls**
PREPARATION TIME **20 minutes, plus**
20 minutes resting time
COOKING TIME **10 minutes**

30g wheat starch
75ml boiling water
40g brown sugar
195ml cold water
150g glutinous rice flour, sifted
3 teaspoons baking powder, sifted
1 tablespoon vegetable oil
100g red bean paste
150g white sesame seeds (untoasted)
300ml vegetable oil, for deep-frying

1 Combine the wheat starch and boiling water in a bowl and mix to a stiff dough. Cover with clingfilm and set aside for 10 minutes.

2 Combine the sugar with the 120ml cold water in a saucepan and stir over a high heat until the sugar dissolves. Remove from the heat and set aside to cool.

3 In a separate bowl, combine the glutinous rice flour, baking powder and vegetable oil with the remaining 75ml cold water. Add the wheat starch dough and knead with your hands until both doughs are thoroughly combined. Return the dough to the bowl, cover with clingfilm and set aside to rest at room temperature for 20 minutes.

4 Meanwhile, wet your hands and shape the red bean paste into 12 even-sized balls. Sprinkle the sesame seeds on a plate ready for coating the balls later. Roll the dough into a long log shape and divide into 2 equal portions. Cut each log into 6 pieces. Roll each piece of dough into a ball and flatten with the palm of your hand into approx. 4cm diameter discs. Using your thumb, press an indent into each piece of dough and insert a ball of red bean paste inside. Draw up the dough around the paste to enclose it fully. Wet the balls in a bowl of water and drop them into the sesame seeds, coating them well on all sides. Roll the sesame-coated ball with your hands to press in the sesame seeds all around the ball.

5 Heat the oil in a wok to 180°C over a high heat. (To test the temperature, place a wooden chopstick in the oil: if bubbles appear around the chopstick the oil is hot enough.) To cook the sesame balls, lower them into the hot oil and fry them for 8–10 minutes until golden brown. Drain on kitchen paper. Serve hot.

Sweet Dumplings
馬蹄

This is a wonderful dim sum to enjoy during Chinese New Year. My mother loves making this with us as a family the night before and we enjoy these sweet dumplings for breakfast. They are circular and symbolise the unity of the family on this very important day. They generally taste very bland to counter the sweetness of the soup.

MAKES **36**
PREPARATION TIME **20 minutes**
COOKING TIME **20 minutes**

300ml water
5cm piece of fresh root ginger,
   peeled and slightly pounded
50g caster sugar
For the dumpling wrappers
240g glutinous rice flour
200ml water

1 First prepare the syrup. Put the water and ginger in a medium saucepan over a high heat and bring to the boil. Cook for 10 minutes, then add the sugar and simmer for a further 5 minutes. Set aside and reheat when the dough balls have cooked.

2 Sift the glutinous rice flour into a large bowl and gradually add the water to form a soft dough. Knead for 5 minutes till the mixture is fully combined.

3 Shape the dough into small round balls by rolling them between the palms. Place the dough balls on a baking tray lined with baking parchment.

4 Heat a medium saucepan half-filled with water over a high heat. Bring to the boil and add the dough balls. Cook for 5 minutes until they have floated to the surface.

5 Meanwhile, reheat the ginger syrup over a medium heat.

6 To serve, scoop the cooked dough balls into the hot syrup and serve in bowls.

Nian Gao with Water Chestnuts

馬蹄糕

This cake, known as Nian Gao, takes its name from a Chinese myth that I loved hearing as a child. In Ancient China, there was a monster called Nian who lived in a cave in the mountain. Most of the year it would stay up the mountain, hunting animals for food, but during the winter, when all the animals were hibernating, Nian was forced to come down to the village in search of humans to satisfy his hunger. Many people lived in fear of Nian until a smart villager, named Gao, decided to take matters into his own hands. Assuming Nian would come down from the mountain and start hunting again, Gao prepared some pastry and put some out in front of every home in the village. When Nian came down the mountain, it could not find any humans to eat and so the monster started feasting on the pastry instead. When Nian's stomach was full, it went back up the mountain – at which point the villagers came out from their houses and celebrated their survival. From then on, the villagers made rice pastry every winter to prevent Nian from eating them. Since Gao invented the rice pastry, the villagers named the rice pastry 'Nian Gao'. During Chinese New Year, families traditionally make this cake for relatives who come to visit or they take it with them when visiting their families. It has a rubbery texture and a slightly sweet taste, in theory to sweeten the year ahead. The symbol for cake in Chinese sounds like 'rising' and symbolises rising prosperity. I hope you and your families enjoy their Nian Gao and have a year of sweet prosperity ahead!

SERVES **4 pieces**
PREPARATION TIME **15 minutes**
COOKING TIME **45 minutes, plus**
cooling and 1 hour chilling

200ml boiling water
100g water chestnut flour
300g glutinous rice flour
2 teaspoons potato starch
2 teaspoons vegetable oil, plus extra
   for greasing and frying
50g caster sugar
50g soft light brown sugar
10 water chestnuts, chopped into
   small pieces

You will need a 20cm loaf tin, greased
with a little oil and lined with
greaseproof paper

1 Pour 100ml boiling water into a mixing bowl. Add the water chestnut flour, glutinous rice flour, potato starch and oil and stir well with a wooden spoon to form a thick paste.
2 Place the remaining 100ml boiling water in a heavy-based saucepan and add both sugars. Set the pan over a medium heat and stir to dissolve the sugar. Remove the pan from the heat and stir in the chopped water chestnuts. Scoop in the flour mixture and mix to a smooth batter. Pour the batter into the prepared tin.
3 Fill a wok with water so that it is just over one-quarter full. Set a round cake rack in the centre, cover with a lid and bring to the boil over a high heat. Place the cake inside the bamboo steamer on top of the wok and steam for 40 minutes over a high heat until the mixture is solid in appearance. Carefully remove the cake from the wok and transfer to the fridge to cool for 1 hour.
4 To serve, turn the cake out of the tin and slice into 4 even slabs. Heat a wok or frying pan over a high heat, add 1 tablespoon of vegetable oil and pan-fry the slices of cake for 2 minutes on each side, then serve.

 LISA'S TIP Blend the chestnut flour with water as you would with cornflour. Give it a good stir before mixing it into the hot liquid to ensure that it is evenly mixed.

Tea

Tea plays an interchangeable part in Chinese cuisine and even the phrase 'let's go for dim sum' can be rephrased as 'let's go for yum char' (which translated literally means to drink tea). There are many different types of Chinese tea – all are good to aid digestion and eliminate the excess oil from the food.

Jasmine

The most popular tea is jasmine tea, which is made by sprinkling jasmine flowers over green tea leaves. The fragrant blossoms are picked and mixed with the green tea according to traditional tea-scenting techniques. The tea absorbs the fragrant essence of the fresh jasmine, making the pearls sweet and aromatic. Jasmine tea is said to reduce nervous tension, decrease saturated fat in the body and increase circulation. Jasmine Dragon Pearl Tea is denser than other teas, so 1–2 teaspoons for a teapot is all that is required. Its name actually means 'common tea' and Jasmine Dragon is a staple in most Chinese households.

Oolong

Oolong tea is produced using a unique process that includes withering the plant under the strong sun and oxidation before curling and twisting. Oolong has a full, rich and slightly smoky flavour with a lingering citrus aftertaste and a characteristic cassia aroma.

Gunpowder
平綠

Gunpowder tea, which is more appropriately called 'Zhu Cha' in Pinyin, is commonly known as 'pearl' tea in China. Gunpowder tea gets its name because of its method of manufacture, which involves rolling it into tiny balls that resemble gunpowder pellets.

Chrysanthemum
菊花

Chrysanthemum tea is perfect when you want a caffeine-free day as this is just dried chrysanthemum flowers in hot water.

Tea Etiquette

Chinese people practise tea drinking etiquette not only during dim sum meals but also during other types of Chinese meals as well.

It is customary to pour tea for others before filling one's own cup during a meal. When pouring tea for people on one's left side, the right hand should be used to hold the teapot and vice-versa. A common custom among the Cantonese is to thank the person pouring the tea by tapping your finger on the table – the bent index finger (if you are single), or the index and middle finger (if you are married). This custom is said to be analogous to the ritual of bowing to someone in appreciation. The origin of this gesture is described anecdotally: an unidentified Emperor went to yum char with his friends, outside the palace. Not wanting to attract attention to himself, the Emperor was disguised. While at yum char, the Emperor poured his companion some tea, which was a great honour. The companion, not wanting to give away the Emperor's identity in public by bowing, instead tapped his index and middle finger on the table as a sign of appreciation.

This ritual is a timesaver, given the number of times tea is poured during a meal – especially in loud restaurants or lively company when an individual might be speaking to someone else or have food in their mouth when they are being served. If a diner does not wish to have the refill being offered at that time, the fingers are used to 'wave off' or politely decline more tea. This does not preclude taking more fresh hot tea at a later time during the meal.

Leaving the lid balanced on the side of the teapot is a common way of attracting a server's attention, and indicates a silent request that the teapot be refilled.

Iced Tea
冰茶

Tea has a history going back 5,000 years, but iced tea only started to become popular as a beverage when the world figured out how to preserve ice in the 17th century. Iced tea is the perfect way to enjoy a refreshing drink and quench your thirst. We like to prepare it in advance and serve it as a delicious alternative to juice or soda. It takes very little preparation and can be drunk plain or spruced up with different fresh fruit.

   Our grandmother told me that iced tea was first discovered by a Commissioner of Tea for India at the St Louis World's Fair in 1904. Richard Blechynden, a tea plantation owner had prepared some samples of hot tea for the fair attendees but observed that no one was willing to sample them as it was an unusually warm day. Most of the fairgoers were seeking cold drinks, so Mr Blechynden decided to cool down his hot tea and offer it as an alternative. The crowd loved it and that was the beginning of what we know as iced tea. My grandmother loved Mr Blechynden's entrepreneurial spirit and every time she made a jug of iced tea she said a big thank you to Mr B!

PG Tea

This recipe is used as the base for most of the recipes in this section.

Makes 300ml
300ml boiling water
1 PG Tips teabag
1 teaspoon sugar

Combine all the ingredients in a pot and set aside to infuse for 5 minutes. Remove the teabag and set aside to cool. Store in the fridge until needed.

Lemon & Ginseng Iced Tea
檸檬人參茶

25ml ginseng tea
200ml PG Tea (see left)
10 ice cubes
25ml Monin lemon syrup

Prepare the PG Tea and ginseng tea and leave to cool for 15 minutes.
Pour both cooled teas into a tall glass, put in the ice cubes and top up with the lemon syrup. Stir well and enjoy.

Mango & Elderflower Iced Tea
芒果接骨木花冰茶

200ml PG Tea (see left)
10 ice cubes
12ml Monin mango syrup
12ml Monin elderflower syrup

Prepare the PG Tea and leave to cool for 15 minutes.
Pour the cooled tea into a tall glass, add the ice cubes and top up with the mango and elderflower syrup.
Stir well and serve.

Pear Iced Tea
梨子冰茶

200ml PG Tea (see left)
10 ice cubes
25ml Monin pear syrup

Prepare the PG Tea and leave to cool for 15 minutes.
Pour the cooled tea into a tall glass, put in the ice cubes and top up with pear syrup. Stir well and serve.

Iced Green Tea
冰綠茶

100ml boiling water
1 teaspoon green tea leaves
1 teaspoon caster sugar
8 ice cubes

Prepare the green tea by combining the hot water with the green tea leaves. Set aside to infuse for 00 minutes and then strain, discarding the tea leaves. Leave to cool for 15 minutes.
Pour the cooled tea into a tall glass and stir in the sugar to dissolve. Add the ice cubes and serve.

Peach Iced Tea
蜜桃冰茶

200ml PG Tea (see left)
10 ice cubes
25ml Monin peach syrup

Prepare the PG Tea and leave to cool for 15 minutes.
Pour the cooled tea into a tall glass, add the ice cubes and top up with the peach syrup. Stir well and enjoy.

Sweet & Sour Sauce

This sauce can be used either as a dipping sauce, a marinade or as a sauce to serve alongside individual recipes.

MAKES **250ml**
PREPARATION TIME **10 minutes**
COOKING TIME **10 minutes**

2 tablespoons tomato ketchup
200ml cold water
100g granulated sugar
75ml white wine vinegar
3 slices of lemon
3 slices of fresh root ginger
1 tablespoon potato starch

Combine all the ingredients except the potato starch in a small saucepan and bring to the boil over a high heat. Add the potato starch and stir vigorously to thicken the sauce. Remove the pan from the heat and set aside to cool. Store in a sealed container in the fridge and use within 2 weeks.

Sweet Chilli Sauce

An exciting concoction of fresh red chillies mixed with garlic and vinegar that tickles the tongue. Perfect for livening up stir-fries, noodles or salads, or on the side as a zingy dip.

MAKES **250ml**
PREPARATION TIME **15 minutes**
COOKING TIME **10 minutes**

4 long red chillies, finely chopped
3 garlic cloves
50ml white wine vinegar
100g granulated sugar
200ml cold water
1 tablespoon salt
1 tablespoon potato starch

Blend all the ingredients except the potato starch in a blender. Pour the mixture into a small saucepan and bring to the boil over a high heat. Add the potato starch and stir vigorously to thicken the sauce. Remove the pan from the heat and set aside to cool. Store in a sealed container in the fridge and use within 2 weeks.

Barbecue Sauce

A thick, fruity sauce that evokes memories of heady evenings. Perfect as a dip with prawn crackers and other snacks, or as a marinade for meats.

MAKES **450ml**
PREPARATION TIME **10 minutes**
COOKING TIME **10 minutes**

300ml tomato ketchup
200ml cold water
125ml red wine vinegar
300g brown sugar
1 teaspoon Worcestershire sauce
2½ teaspoons mustard powder
2 teaspoons paprika
1 teaspoon salt
1 teaspoon freshly ground black pepper

Combine all the ingredients in a small saucepan and whisk well until the spices have distributed evenly and the sugar has dissolved. Bring to the boil then remove the pan from the heat and set aside to cool.
Store in a sealed container in the fridge and use within 2 weeks.

Hoisin
Sauce

Hoisin sauce is a thick, sweet and salty sauce that is commonly found in many Chinese restaurants around the world accompanying the famous Peking Duck dish. It is a classic Chinese sauce that contains soya beans, sesame oil, sugar, and spices. It is often referred to as the Chinese Barbecue sauce as the spices added give it a distinctive rich flavour. I hope you enjoy making hoisin sauce at home to go with your duck and other stir-fry dishes.

MAKES **approx. 250ml**
PREPARATION TIME **15 minutes**
COOKING TIME **5 minutes**

**6 tablespoons minced soya bean
paste
6 tablespoons water
2 tablespoons light soy sauce
1 tablespoon dark soy sauce
2 tablespoons black bean paste
3 tablespoons brown sugar
2 tablespoons white vinegar
2 garlic cloves, finely chopped
2 teaspoons sesame oil
2 teaspoons chilli sauce
½ teaspoon white pepper
1 tablespoon potato starch**

Place all the ingredients in a mixing bowl and whisk together until they form a thick sauce.

Pour the combined sauce into a small saucepan over a medium heat and simmer for 5 minutes, stirring continuously. The sauce will turn a rich brown colour.

Pour the cooked sauce into a dipping bowl and serve. Store in a sealed container in the fridge and use within 4 weeks.